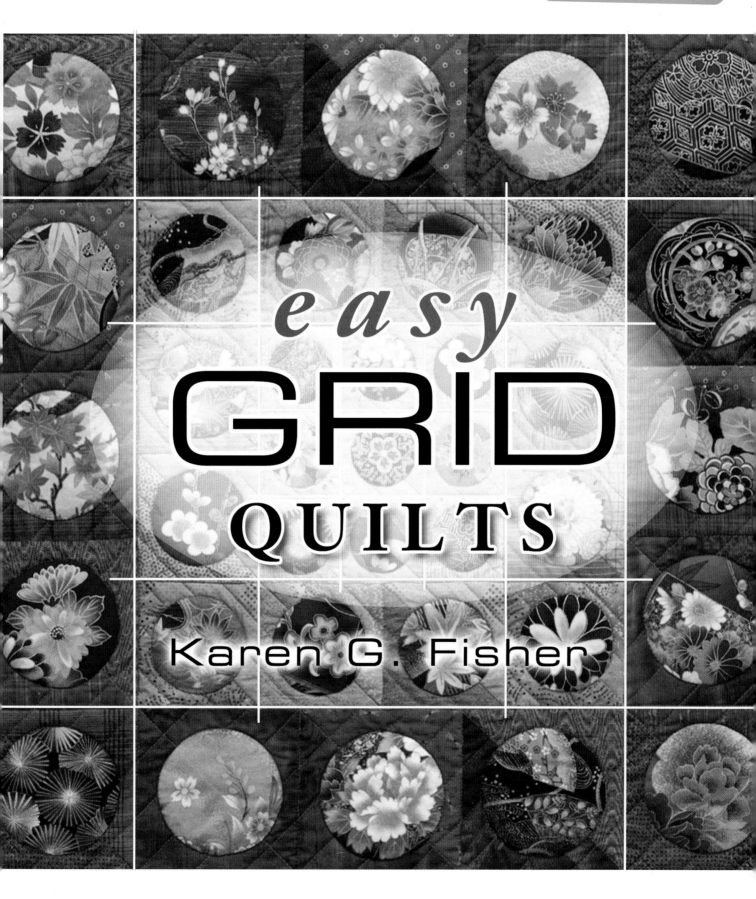

easy GRID QUILTS

Karen G. Fisher

AQS Publishing

Located in Paducah, Kentucky, the American Quilter's Society (AQS) is dedicated to promoting the accomplishments of today's quilters. Through its publications and events, AQS strives to honor today's quiltmakers and their work and to inspire future creativity and innovation in quiltmaking.

Executive Editor: Andi Milam Reynolds
Senior Editor: Linda Baxter Lasco
Graphic Design: Lynda Smith
Copy Editor: Chrystal Abhalter
Cover Design: Michael Buckingham
Photography: Charles R. Lynch

Library of Congress Cataloging-in-Publication Data

Fisher, Karen G.
 Easy grid quilts / by Karen G. Fisher.
    pages cm
 Summary: "Fourteen modern, sophisticated quilt projects based on five basic grid concepts. Teaches how to use focus fabrics and color to achieve complex-looking results from simple squares and rectangles sewn together. Optional machine appliqué for embellishment and detailed quilting design suggestions complete the book"--Provided by publisher.
 ISBN 978-1-60460-013-1
 1. Quilting--Patterns. 2. Grids (Crisscross patterns) in art. I. Title.
 TT835.F5667 2012
 746.46--dc23
                2012004138

I wish to acknowledge the ongoing friendship and support of the Tucson Quilters Guild. The lectures and workshops I have been privileged to attend through the guild have helped me to expand my repertoire of skills and continue to enrich my appreciation of quilting in all its variety. A special thanks to the Mona Lisa Bee, a close group of friends and quilters who keep me grounded in the charitable traditions of quilters nationwide, and to Deanna Juvera who first understood my "Matrix" idea.

I give special credit to my granddaughter, Emily, who really got me started on quilting, and who even helped me find the fabrics for one of the quilts in this book.

Finally, to my husband, Howard, who has been my most objective critic and who has put up with my quilting overtaking our house.

Table of Contents

Introduction to the Basic Grid Concept and Formats

Most traditional quilts are based on grids. Some quilts have one repeating shape, such as charm quilts, Grandmother's Flower Garden, and Lone Star quilts. Quilts with a repeating block may have a block and sashing grid. Each block is broken down into a smaller grid, and secondary patterns/grids often form as the blocks are assembled.

I tended not to use these formal arrangements until I began a series of quilts that explore color in a very structured way. Those explorations came from my lifelong art background and from my interest in the patterns formed by mathematical progressions. Though I'm not a mathematician, I discovered the patterns that could be created using math were very rich, and I found their formality extremely pleasing.

These grids are not just patterns for making specific quilts. Instead, I hope to excite you about new ways to use and arrange color to achieve beautiful, individualized quilts. Use my grids to explore your own love of color and fabric and pattern.

Graduated Grid

At quilt shows, I always enjoyed the look of quilts that had more than one size of blocks. They would often go from areas of small blocks in the center, to medium size blocks, to large blocks around the edge. These were generally large bed quilts, so the most detailed areas would be seen most clearly when the quilt was laid out on the bed.

Some of the size combinations were immediately clear. For example, 3", 6", and 9" blocks form a steady progression and can be fit together as modular units. The only problem is that these quilts can get very

big very fast! I make mostly wall pieces, so I wanted to control the size of my quilts and still have various sized blocks. When the solution came to me, it was so elegant that I had to start playing with the design possibilities immediately.

While I cannot imagine that I am the first person to discover this size and pattern progression, I have not seen it anywhere else. Even a friend who is a mathematician had no name for it, but he found it very interesting. The basic idea is that if you start with four 1" blocks/squares in the center, you can evenly surround them with 2" blocks. These can be evenly surrounded with 3" blocks, then 4" blocks, and so on. The numbers work as far up as I have tried to go (to infinity?), but by the time the progression reaches a 10" block you have a 110" square quilt—a king-size!

Quilts based on the Graduated grid are on pages 17-33 and in the Gallery on pages 72, 73, 75, and 76.

SPIRAL IN, SPIRAL OUT, detail, made with the Graduated grid. Full quilt on page 76.

Double Sudoku

When Sudoku puzzles became popular, many quilters thought of converting colors to numbers and creating a quilt. A basic single Sudoku puzzle is really only nine Nine-Patch blocks, and if they are all run together, they form a simple, visually random arrangement of 81 squares. I made double and triple Sudoku layouts for more visual interest.

Quilts based on the Double Sudoku grid are on pages 34–45 and in the Gallery on page 74.

SUNDAY MORNING SUDOKU II, detail, made with a Double Sudoku grid. Full quilt on page 34.

Miriam's Grid

At first glance, many people think the quilts based on Miriam's grid are bargello quilts, but the pieces change size in both directions, rather than being made from identical strips that are shifted vertically. Most of the versions I have made with this grid use four to five values of groups of colors. PRISM II uses 15 colors that follow the color wheel, plus three extra to add variety and value.

Quilts based on Miriam's grid are on pages 46–52.

PRISM II, detail, made with Miriam's grid. Full quilt on page 52.

Triaxial Color Grid

Before I became interested in quilting, I did ceramics. I took several semesters of classes at the university level, and along the way I learned many glaze-making techniques.

One method used a triaxial blending chart to develop new glazes. The chart outlined how to blend three ingredients in different percentages by weight. I wondered if I could use three colors of fabric, mix them by percentages for each block in a grid, and develop a new way to work with color. I chose three of my favorite colors—red, golden yellow, and turquoise—and went to work.

As that first trial piece came together, I was delighted with how the color moved across the 64-square grid. That first experiment became part of the larger quilt

AND THEN THERE'S RED. I especially enjoy using this grid as a background for appliqué. This pattern is also very graphic by itself.

Quilts based on the Triaxial Color grid are on pages 55–62 and in the Gallery on pages 74, 76, and 77.

AND THEN THERE'S RED, detail, made with a Triaxial Color grid. Full quilt on page 76.

Matrix

Matrix uses the simplest grid of all—a square inside another square. What makes it exciting is the flow of color from low contrast to high contrast areas with contrast both in value and color.

My first Matrix quilt was inspired by my memory of mathematical matrices used for addition and multiplication. Although math was never my strong suit, I remembered my fascination with the patterns of numbers that formed across the matrix as the numbers were combined. I wanted to see what would happen if I used colors instead of numbers.

I tried several ideas for combining two-colored squares, but I was also constantly aware that I would need a way to keep 676 little blocks organized. Yes— you read it right—the first Matrix quilt used twenty-six colors, so it had 676 blocks (26 x 26)!

When I settled on the square within a square idea, I tried both piecing and appliqué construction. I settled on hand appliqué because it gave me the look I wanted, it was the easiest to organize and construct, and the inner squares could have lots of variety in shape and size (see detail—the centers are not all identical, nor are they perfect squares).

Quilts based on the Matrix grid are on pages 63–68 and in the Gallery on page 73.

MATRIX: VI: 15², detail, made with the Matrix grid. Full quilt on page 63.

From Falling in Love with Fabric to Building a Useable Stash

My journey to quilting began a long time ago. I was introduced to sewing in junior high school. I made a few of my own clothes, but my main interest, even then, was really art. In high school, fabric and art came together in a series of church banners I made, mostly by hand, from satins, velvets, and elegant trims.

I got my first job in a fabric store. It was the 1970s and polyester was king! We may shudder at the memory of double knit leisure suits, but polyester was wonderful to learn to sew on. I became fearless, using complex patterns and taking advantage of the knowledge of women who were lifelong seamstresses. And there were silks. China had opened for trade, and I bought yards and yards of silk brocade to make my wedding dress, even though I didn't have a boyfriend at the time! I experimented on silks, wools, fake furs, and any unusual fabrics I could find. I loved them all.

However, it was a sad time for cotton fabrics. The cottons in the store were of poor quality and not particularly attractive. No matter how much their prices were marked down, nobody seemed to want them. Even so, in 1976 and 1979, when my daughters were born, I dutifully made each of them a quilt from a pattern that used only three different fabrics.

In the 1980s, I made wedding dresses, Renaissance costumes, and wonderful formal wear. In 1990, I returned to school full-time and subsequently taught both art and science for a while. Then a little miracle came along that led me back to fabric and sewing.

In 2002, my granddaughter Emily was born. I made a quilt for her and I had so much fun making it that I decided to do more quilting. By then, there were quilt shops and wonderful fabrics available, but even as I started quilting, I bought fabric in very closely coordinated colors. Emily's quilt was made from beautiful hand-dyed pinks and some small-scale pink and green fabrics—a perfect complementary color scheme.

Somewhere in the middle of all this, I made a quilt for my daughter, Miriam, from a modular grid she had designed. We bought solids and marbled fabrics in the colors she wanted. I liked her design so well that I later scaled it down and made it in my own colors, then I modified it and played with it some more.

Next I made my first Matrix quilt, which needed 26 different colors. It was easy to pick the colors I wanted, but it was not easy finding them all in fabric. I was discovering that quilt fabrics, like clothing fabrics, go in and out of season and fashion. The light green I wanted was very difficult to find that year, but two years later I found more than twenty fabrics in the same light green for another piece I was making.

As I developed my quilting style, I built my stash of tone-on-tone fabrics quite deliberately. When I shopped for specific quilts, I added to my stash with any other colors I needed. I occasionally bought printed fabrics, but not very often.

I developed my Triaxial Color grid next, and continued to expand my collection of fabrics. I discovered I only needed to buy quarter yards most of the time because I built whole sections of color from many, many fabrics.

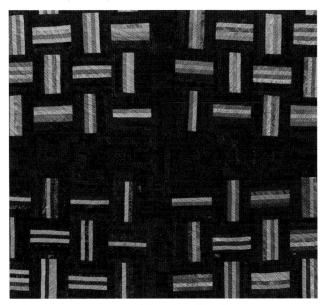

AND THEN THERE'S RED, detail. Full quilt on page 76.

For my first Sudoku quilt, I selected nine analogous colors I liked and added black silk for a neutral. To make the eight- and nine-color assortments I will show later (page 35), I bought small cuts of printed fabrics and pulled the coordinating colors from my stash.

Over time I have also acquired an assortment of neutrals. My black-and-white selections began with a specific quilt, then kept growing. I love metallic prints, so I buy colors with gold whenever I see them, especially black-and-gold and ivory-and-gold prints. They are most often available near Christmas, so I always stock up. I include batiks in my own definition of tone-on-tones and use them often with printed fabrics.

I've made a few quilts based on particular fabric themes, so I would start looking for fabric as soon as the idea began to come together. My assortment of prints is dwarfed by my tone-on-tone collections, but I have African-style fabrics, roses, Southwestern and Mexican fabrics, food fabrics, and lots of star fabrics, all purchased when quilts were in the planning stages. I buy larger cuts of large-scale prints when I will be fussy-cutting fabric. And if I love a big splashy print, I will buy a larger piece of it to make a quilt backing somewhere along the way.

If you are a new quilter, have fun purchasing lots of new fabrics to work with my grid patterns. If you've quilted for a while, your stash will reflect your own style and tastes. If you have colorful prints, select them as beginnings for the Sudoku or Triaxial grids. If your stash is heavy on your favorite colors, pick those to start with, then add whatever new colors you need. If you do need to buy all new fabrics for one of my quilt patterns, you may end up with lots of leftovers. Of course, that can be the best reason to create another quilt!

Color, Color, Color

You will discover that I love bright color and high contrast. While bright, high-contrast quilts are certainly popular, I believe I come by my color sense because I have lived in the Arizona desert most of my life. Pastel colors disappear in bright desert sunlight.

I learned the color wheel in junior high school and I have been actively working with color for more than 40 years. I have a lifetime of practice using color, in art classes in high school and university, in making clothing for clients and family, and finally in quilting. Let me share a bit of what I have learned.

We all have a sense of color—what we like and don't like, what colors make us happy or sad or uncomfortable. When you make a quilt, don't let someone else, including me, talk you into using colors you don't like. If you love a color, use it a lot. Most of my quilts contain red because I love red, but I've learned to place it carefully because it can take over visually. In my quilt SURROUNDED (page 23), the red was toned down with the surrounding purple and blue.

Yellow is also difficult to place. It is both light in value and bright in intensity, so it stands out wherever it is used. It works best if it is meant to be the center of attention, or if it is balanced with more yellow.

PRISM II, detail. Full quilt on page 52.

Orange, between red and yellow, is not as strong as either, but an orange background on a quilt can be overwhelming.

If you know the color wheel, you know that red, orange, and yellow are warm colors, while blues, greens, and violets are cool colors. In general, warm colors stand out, and cool colors recede or blend in. If you don't have a color wheel, buy a simple one

SURROUNDED, detail. Full quilt on page 23.

as a reference tool and get comfortable with the basics. Complementary and triadic color groups can provide high contrast, while analogous colors will give a softer blending.

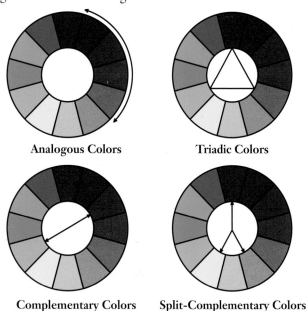

Analogous Colors **Triadic Colors**

Complementary Colors **Split-Complementary Colors**

I find many commercially available color wheels confusing, because they have so much overlapping information. These simple ones illustrate basic analogous, triadic, complementary, and split-complementary color groups.

Black can look very dynamic, or it can overwhelm a quilt, so I rarely use solid black. I don't use it with a print, unless there is black in the print itself. I use black-on-black or black-and-gold fabrics to soften the visual impact of that darkest value. I don't use pure white plain fabric, either. I use white-on-white prints or ivory tone-on-tones. I prefer off-white, and my favorites are ivory-and-gold prints. However, I'm always willing to try something different in a quilt. Green is a color I don't like very much, but it is often the right color to use for the value or color contrast I want, so it shows up often in my work.

When you're selecting colors, remember each color family has a full range of values and intensities. "Red" goes all the way from the palest pink to deep burgundy, and from soft dusty rose to fluorescent. "Green" includes forest green and mint green along with khaki, olive, and Kelly green. So start with the colors you love and let your quilt projects build from there.

Paint chip samples (at top) can truly show the whole range of a particular color family. These reds are from just one manufacturer, yet these samples still don't show the full selection of value and intensity available in just one color. Red fabrics (at bottom) also come in a whole range of colors.

Border Treatments

Spinning Borders

I like to use "spinning" borders to add detail at the corners without mitering. One simple partial seam is all that's needed.

Select your border fabric and width.

Cut each border piece the length of one side *plus* the width of the border *plus* one inch. (Each border piece is a different color so they are easier to see.

Applying a spinning border

Line up border piece A with one edge of the quilt center. The other end will extend beyond the center.

Stitch in place, stopping a few inches before the end on the extended edge.

Attach border pieces B, C, and D in order. Press the seam allowances toward the border.

Stitch the end of border A where it overlaps border D to complete the first seam.

Trim the corners if necessary.

Completed and trimmed spinning border

This treatment was especially effective on ORNAMENTS, page 75.

Making Tucked Borders
Selecting Fabric

Most of the fabrics I use to make tucks are tone-on-tone prints. These hide any irregularities better than solid colors. Some simple prints also work well. Large or very colorful prints can also work—tucking them makes them look like a coordinated fabric to the original piece.

Estimating Yardage for a Simple Border

A full width of standard cotton fabric will tuck down to about 30 inches wide with the density of tucks I like to do.

For example, if I want a 6" border on a quilt that will have a 120" finished perimeter, I need four 30" lengths of tucked fabric, or 24" (just under ¾ yard).

Because there is some distortion while doing the stitching, I always make extra tucked fabric, usually about a quarter yard. Whatever fabric is left over can add wonderful detail to another piece. If you decide to use a tucked border, add ¼ yard to the border yardage requirements.

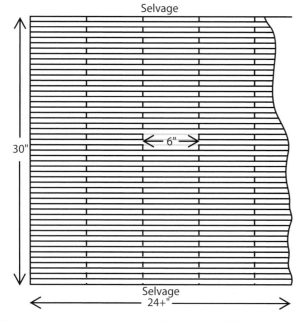

When estimating yardage for a tucked border, note that a full width of fabric, selvage to selvage, will measure about 30" when tucked. You can cut 5–6 – 6" wide panels of tucked fabric from one yard, giving you approximately 150"–180" of tucked border.

It is awkward to work with more than 1 yard of fabric at a time. To make more than 180" of tucked border panels, make it in more than one piece.

Finding and Pressing the Center

Press out the folded center of the fabric—it is rarely the true center. Now fold the fabric, right side out, with the selvages lined up together. The piece of fabric must lie smoothly from selvage to center, no matter what the ends look like. Press this center line with a nice hot steam iron. If the crease does

not seem to be holding, spritz it with a little water and press again. At this point you can square up the ends of your fabric if you desire, but there will be some distortion as you stitch, so you can leave the trimming for later.

Pressing the Rest of the Tucks in Place

Your pressed center fold is your first reference fold (A). One side at a time, bring each selvage edge into the center and carefully line it up with the fold. Remember the folds all must go in the same direction—they do not go back and forth like a fan. Once you have the selvage and center lined up, press that fold with lots of steam. Then do the other side. Your fabric will now be pressed in fourths (B).

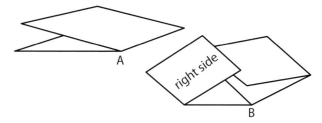

Now bring each edge up to the quarter folds and press in place. Line up each edge with the OPPOSITE quarter fold to make lines on either side of the center. Now the fabric is divided into eighths (C).

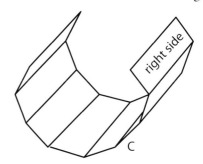

For narrower and narrower tucks, continue to divide each width in half: bring each edge into the first pressed line and press the new fold in place. Then move the edge up to the appropriate fold and press again. This takes a bit of practice, but it will make sense as you do it. Subdivide your fabric as many times as necessary to get the size tucks you want.

Stitching the Tucks

Decide how deep you want your tucks. For a larger quilt, they can be up to ¼" deep. For smaller quilts, you will probably want closely spaced tucks and a narrower finished width. Use matching or contrasting thread, depending on the look you want.

To stitch accurately, find a spot on your presser foot that you can line up with easily. I use my zigzag foot and plate, and I can change the needle position to get a tuck depth that I like (D).

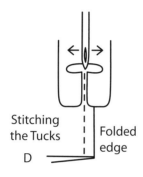

Stitching the Tucks

Folded edge

D

Start from one end of the fabric, and stitch all tucks from the same side. Most sewing machine stitches are not identical top and bottom, and all the tucks should match. Make sure you have a full bobbin, so you don't run out of thread in the middle of a row.

Pressing the Tucks

Lay the fabric, tucks up, on your ironing board (E). Make sure your surface is not too slippery. Starting at one end, steam press all the tucks in the same direction. Turn the fabric over and press again. Make sure you apply enough pressure to "push" the tucks all the way out.

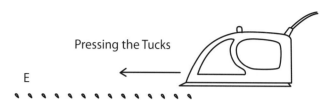

Pressing the Tucks

E

Finally, to get the fabric really flat, spray it with a little water, and press it again. In this last step, make sure the tucks are nicely parallel. "Eyeballing" is usually enough. If you want to use a ruler, you can, but minor imperfections won't really show.

Using Tucked Fabric

When pressing seams, press away from the tucked pieces, so that the tucks stay flat in the seam. Tucked fabric also works well on the bias, because all the stitching helps stabilize the fabric.

When quilting across the tucks, be careful not to push them over backwards. I have had large quilts done by longarm quilters who had no trouble with the tucks. One quilter did an allover pattern over the tucks, and the other quilter stitched parallel to them to accent them.

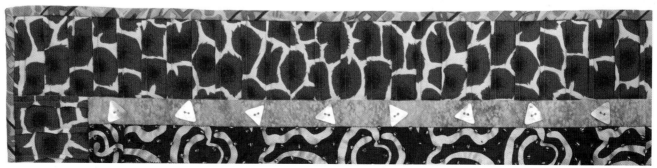

Twiga III: Savannah Sunlight, detail, showing a tucked border. Full quilt on page 77.

Quilting

We all know a quilt isn't a quilt until it's quilted. Depending on your skill level, your machine, quilt size, and time constraints, you may choose to do your own quilting, or you may work with a professional quilter. I start thinking about all these things as soon as I begin a quilt, rather than leaving the decision until the last moment.

Early in my quilting life, I was lucky enough to go to the International Quilt Festival in Houston. If I had not gone when I did, my quilting might have developed very differently, but I fell in love with the look of very dense, non-traditional allover machine quilting. While I also enjoy beautiful hand quilting and traditional designs done on machine, my own work, inspired by the work I saw then, is still very densely stitched.

I have done both my own quilting and had it done by others. When I do my own quilting, I often have a very clear idea of the look I want, and it is rarely translatable to another person. I rarely plan my quilting—I figure it out as I go along. I often work diagonally across the surface, ignoring any block arrangements. I like spirals, big sweeping curves, and very dense quilting, sometimes as close as every ¼" across most of the surface.

PRISM II, detail, with swirling, allover quilting. Full quilt on page 52.

When I work with a professional quilter, I either tell her what I want done (such as in MATRIX: COLOR SYNERGY, quilted by Nubin Jensen, page 66), or I let the quilter rely on her own expertise and style (see TWIGA III: SAVANNAH SUNLIGHT, quilted by Mary Vaneecke, page 77).

I also do lots of stitch-in-the-ditch, using an open-toe zigzag foot so I can see exactly where I'm going. I've used blanket and feather stitching for quilting, which outlines and quilts an area in one step. At other times, I've echo-quilted around shapes, then let the "echo" expand and change direction to become the background.

VISIT TO PROVENCE, detail, with circles that echo the appliquéd circles. Full quilt on page 26.

If you have worked with a professional longarm quilter, you may have seen the amazing designs that are available for custom work on traditional quilts. However, I feel that many of the grid quilts lend themselves well to allover designs, that, on the plus side, can be less expensive to have done.

Mary Vaneecke, a good friend and award-winning longarm quilter here in Tucson, worked with me on picking some wonderful allover designs to enhance my quilts. If you look closely, you will see spirals (DREAMING OF NEW MEXICO), chilies (CHILE CON SUDOKU), music notation (SUNDAY MORNING SUDOKU II) roses (GARLAND), stars (SURROUNDED),

and leaves (KALEIDOSCOPE GARDEN) that flow from edge to edge in continuous patterns. In each case, we looked at thread colors—often multi-colored—that worked with the quilt top, and Mary manipulated the scale to an appropriate size for the quilt. The finished quilts, with their rich combinations of color and texture, are delightful.

DREAMING OF NEW MEXICO, detail. Full quilt on page 19.

CHILE CON SUDOKU, detail. Full quilt on page 40.

SUNDAY MORNING SUDOKU II, detail. Full quilt on page 34.

GARLAND, detail. Full quilt on page 55.

SURROUNDED, detail. Full quilt on page 23.

KALEIDOSCOPE GARDEN, detail. Full quilt on page 73.

So before you do your quilting, or have it done, be aware of all the wonderful options available to you. The right quilting can transform your finished quilt from ordinary to exceptional.

Graduated Grid

As I have developed this grid idea, one of the things I have enjoyed is being able to use differently scaled fabrics to full advantage. So whether you use fabrics from a coordinated group or select your own, there are areas in the pattern that need the very smallest scale prints and other areas that can show off larger scale fabrics. In the Graduated grid, fussy-cutting can make one fabric look like many. Directional fabrics, such as stripes and plaids, can also be placed to great advantage because you can decide which way you want them to go as the design develops.

In the Graduated grid, you start with four 1" blocks/squares in the center, then evenly surround them with 2" blocks. These are then evenly surrounded with 3" blocks, then 4" blocks, and so on. The three Graduated grid projects vary the size and arrangement of the blocks, but the basic idea is the same.

Cutting the Blocks

I like to use square rulers in the sizes of the blocks I need to cut because it is easier to center the motifs before cutting the squares. The sizes I use are 2½", 3½", 4½", 5½", and 6½". For the 1½" squares I use the smallest ruler I have. The 5½" size can be hard to find. You do not need all these sizes as long as you can clearly see through your rulers to center the image you want to highlight.

I generally do not cut all the blocks/squares at once. I start in the very center and assemble the 1", 2", and 3" blocks first. I then audition different fabrics for scale, imagery, and color to see where I want to use them.

Using Different Kinds of Symmetry

Most traditional quilts use simple side-to-side (like the symmetry of a face) and top-to-bottom symmetry. I use both of these plus diagonal symmetry and

rotational symmetry to add interest to my color/block arrangements.

Diagonal symmetry is just what it sounds like—pieces match diagonally across from each other. This can be corner-to-corner or at a lesser angle.

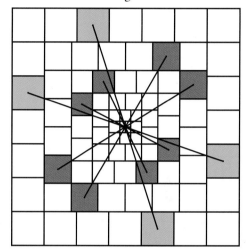

Diagonal symmetry

Rotational symmetry means the same progression of fabrics repeats as you go around a shape. For example, if a round of squares (an arrangement of same-size squares around a previously pieced center) has twenty squares (the 5" blocks), and you have four fabrics, then every fifth block/square will be the same. I have discovered that rotational symmetry is most interesting when the total number of blocks can be divided by an odd number.

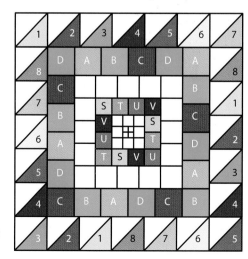

Rotational symmetry in the third, fifth, and sixth rounds

Graduated Grid

Make extra copies of this basic layout and use colored pencils to try different arrangements.

Assembly Hint: If you are not able to sew your blocks together immediately, keep a camera handy to photograph your fabric arrangement.

The Basic Grid:

DREAMING OF NEW MEXICO

42" x 42", made by the author, quilted by Mary Vaneecke

Karen G. Fisher Easy Grid Quilts **19**

This pattern is designed for theme fabrics in multiple scales. It has no sashing—the blocks are visually separated from each other as the scale changes. You will discover there are very few seams to match—only the very corner blocks actually line up. The smallest blocks need tiny pieces of fabric or very small-scale fabric if you want to fussy-cut images.

I used Western and Mexican themed fabrics because I had so many and they are readily available. Other ideas could work as well such as Africa, flowers, cats, food, or sports. Use fabrics that highlight imagery from your part of the country, your favorite part of the world, your ethnic background, or a hobby. This is also a fun piece to use fussy-cutting to highlight the images in some of your fabrics. Start with fabric left over from other projects. If you already have a good-sized fabric stash, you probably have many fabrics in similar themes or colors, because we all have favorites.

Fabric Requirements

You will need 20 to 24 fabrics (the sample quilt has 20). Many prints have enough variety in them that different areas will read as different fabrics.

You may want more yardage of any large-scale fabrics for fussy cutting. These are the finished sizes of the blocks. Cut sizes are ½" larger.

Total yardages from a variety of fabrics.
Center 1" blocks: scraps
Second round 2" blocks: ⅛ yard
Third round 3" blocks: ¼ yard
Fourth round 4" blocks : ⅜ yard
Fifth round 5" blocks: ½ yard
Sixth round 6" blocks: ¾ – 1 yard
8 of the 24 blocks are Four-Patch blocks
12 motifs for the puffy appliqué (see the skulls between

the 5th and 6th rounds): These could come from one of your large-scale fabrics or from a separate fabric. How much you need depends on the repeat of the design. Simple shapes with soft curves work best.
Puffy appliqué backing: ¼ yard
Thin batting for puffy appliqué: ½ yard
Heat-and-bond product: ½ yard of your favorite product
Batting: 50" x 50"
Backing: 3 yards
Binding: ½ yard

At least 5 of the fabrics should be "fillers"—stripes or allover patterns. You will need ¼ yard (fat or long cut quarters) for each of these five. The very largest cuts of fabric are 6½" x 6½", so I recommend ½ yard cuts of your largest-scale fabrics.

You will be "Swiss-cheesing" your fabrics, so look at the imagery in your largest prints to make sure you can cut at least 4 squares. The skeleton figures in the outer row fit perfectly in the 6" blocks and I was able to use the fabric quite efficiently.

If the motif is on the diagonal in the fabric, reinforce it with a lightweight, iron-on interfacing. Be aware of the direction you cut and assemble any striped fabrics. Also make sure to use any directional imagery in the direction you want it on the final quilt.

Cutting Instructions

Center: 4 – 1½" x 1½" squares
Round 1: 8 – 2½" x 2½" squares
Round 2: 12 – 3½" x 3½" squares
Round 3: 16 – 4½" x 4½" squares
Round 4: 20 – 5½" x 5½" squares
Round 5: 16 – 6½" x 6½" squares and 32 – 3½" x 3½" squares (for the Four-Patch blocks)

Divide your fabric into groups based on scale, and give yourself a variety of colors in each group for visual interest. Also determine if any of your fabrics can be cut to show off different areas so that it looks like you have more fabrics.

In the sample, several of the fabrics are allover prints that are not fussy-cut or directional. Fabric C is used differently in three different places, and fabric O is used twice. Fabrics P, O, and C are used directionally, either pointing out from the center, or going around the center.

This cutting guide and layout are simply possible ways to group your fabrics.

A and B: 2 – 1½" squares each (4 total)
C and D: 4 – 2½" squares each (8 total)
E, F and G: 4 – 3½" squares each (12 total)
H, I, J, and K: 4 – 4½" squares each (16 total)
L, M, N, O, and P: 4 – 5½" squares each (20 total)
Q, R, and C (two different fussy-cut motifs): 4 – 6½" squares each (16 total)
The remaining 8 – 6½" squares are Four-Patch blocks made as follows:
N and K: 4 – 3½" squares each; make 2
S and O: 8 – 3½" squares each; make 4
T and E: 4 – 3½" squares each; make 2

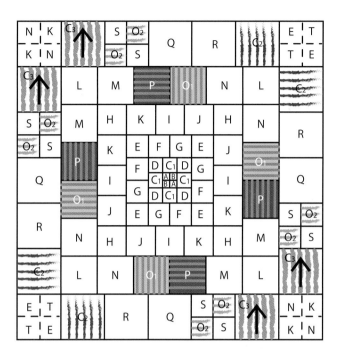

Quilt Assembly

Assemble the quilt from the center out.

Start with the 4 – 1½" squares and make a Four-Patch block.

Round 1: Add a 2½" square to two opposite sides of the Four-Patch center.

Make 2 units of 3 – 2½" squares each and add to the top and bottom of the center unit.

Note: The number of squares added to the sides and to the top and bottom increases by one on each of the subsequent rounds.

Round 2: Join 2 squares of the next size and add to the sides. Then make 2 units of the remaining squares of that size and add to the top and bottom.

Rounds 3 & 4: Continue in this manner, adding units of blocks to the sides, then to the top and bottom.

Round 5: Make 8 Four-Patch blocks with the 3½" squares. Distribute around the center with the 16 plain 6½" squares. Join the blocks and squares into units and add to the quilt.

Making Puffy Appliqués

Cut out 12 images with about ½" extra seam allowance. Cut 2 pieces of fusible web, thin batting, and backing.

Fuse the images to thin batting.

Fuse the backing fabric to the other side of the batting. Trim the shape/image, leaving about ⅛" around the edge.

Zigzag around the entire motif with matching or contrasting thread, depending on the finish you want.

Go around twice to get better coverage if necessary.

Bury the ends of the thread in the batting. Fasten the finished puffy appliqué to your finished quilt with buttons or beads.

Fasten the appliqués to the quilt between Rounds 4 and 5.

Just a note about the skeleton and skull imagery on the quilt: The Day of the Dead, or *Día de los Muertos*, is a very special day celebrated just after Halloween in Mexico and the southwestern United States. The holiday is for celebrating and acknowledging that we still love and miss family members and friends who have passed away. On this day, graveyards are cleaned and decorated, there are parades, and special foods including decorated sugar skulls are prepared for both the living and dead to enjoy. The attitude of the day is very positive, as people express to their lost loved ones, "We love you, we miss you, come back and party for a day with us."

Pieced Blocks:
SURROUNDED

42" x 42", made by the author, quilted by Mary Vaneecke

As soon as I had designed the basic grid, I started looking for variations of it. What if I made the blocks with the same number of pieces as the size of the block? The 1" block with one piece, the 2" block with two pieces, 3" with three pieces, and so on, so as the blocks get larger, they become more complex.

With more complex blocks, the fabrics became simpler. I returned to my favorite fabrics—tone-on-tones. I chose a group of colors I liked, basically following the color wheel, and raided my stash. The central 1" blocks are two hues of yellow-green. Next comes yellow, also in two hues, then orange, red, lavender, and blue. Whether you use this same group of colors or another, make sure your strongest color is in the 4" block group. With this placement, the blocks both inside and outside the 4" group will help balance and contain that strongest color.

Fabric Requirements

For all the colors, fabric quantities are estimates only. The more fabrics you have in each color, the less you will need of each separate fabric.

For the 1", 2", and 3" blocks: scraps or ⅛ yard *each* of two values

For the 4", 5", and 6" blocks: ¼ yard *each* of two values or pull from your stash

Note: These are the finished sizes of the blocks.

Batting: 50" x 50"
Backing: 3 yards
Binding: ½ yard

Block Cutting & Construction

1" blocks:
Cut 4 – 1½" x 1½" squares

2" blocks:
Cut a total of 8 – 2⅞" x 2⅞" squares

Make 8 half-square triangle units. Trim to measure 2½" x 2½".

3" blocks:
Cut 36 – 1½" x 3½" strips
Join into 3-strip units OR make strip-sets of 3 – 1½" wide WOF strips and cut into 3½" blocks.

4" blocks:
Cut 16 – 5¼" x 5¼" squares
Cut apart using the template pattern on page 25.
Make 16 quarter-square triangle units to measure 4½" x 4½".

5" blocks:
Cut 20 – 6¼" squares
Cut apart using the template pattern on page 25.
Assemble 20 square-in-a-square blocks to measure 5½" x 5½".

6" blocks:
Cut 24 light and 24 dark 6½" x 3½" rectangles and 48 light and 48 dark 3½" x 3½" squares.

Sew the squares on the diagonal to the ends of the rectangles to assemble 48 Flying Geese units. Trim and press. Make 24 blocks of 2 Flying Geese units each, matching the light and dark arrangement of geese and wings.

Press and join the blocks following the assembly diagram. I like to piece each group of one size blocks and add them to the center before moving on to the next size block. This way, I have fewer loose blocks to keep track of at any given point during assembly.

As you can see, this quilt has no extra border, but you are free to add one if that is the look you prefer. The quilting is an allover star design. After quilting, I suggest using one of your interior colors for binding. I used my favorite—red.

Block #4

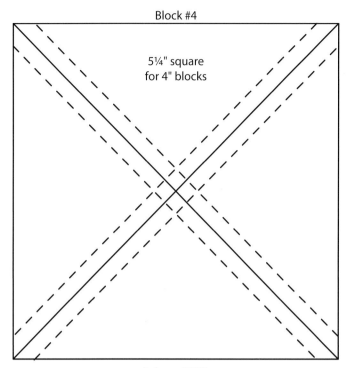

5¼" square
for 4" blocks

Enlarge 150%
Cut apart on solid lines, sew together in pairs,
then sew pairs together into 4 quarter-square triangles

Block #5

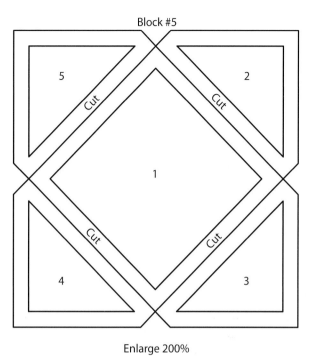

Enlarge 200%
6¼" square for 5" finished block
Cut in 5-square stacks, re-stack pieces, stitch together in order

**SURROUNDED
assembly
diagram**

Circle in a Square:
Visit to Provence

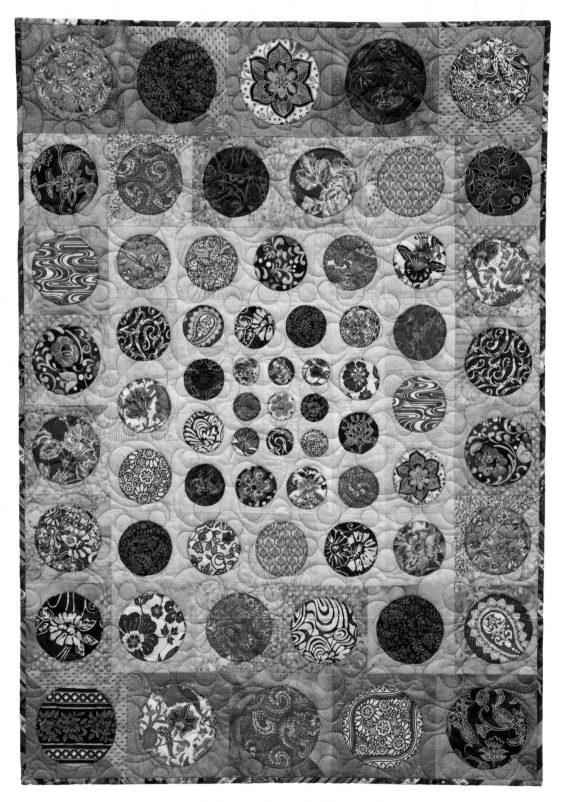

30" x 42", made by the author, quilted by Mary Vaneecke

Karen G. Fisher

The name for this quilt came from the classic combination of yellow, blue, and white—colors that seem to be readily available at all quilt shops. I don't always want to make square quilts, so I simply left the 6" blocks off of two sides to make a rectangle. You will also notice that the center 1" blocks have been replaced by a single 2" block. I felt four tiny little circles would look very crowded.

It's time to try appliqué if you haven't already. Circles are the very simplest shapes to appliqué, and there are many methods that work—by hand or machine, with blanket stitch or satin stitch, with matching or contrasting thread.

Fabric and Cutting Instructions

As with all my quilts, you can start with your stash. A progression of background fabrics from light to dark will give your quilt a lovely glow or luminosity in the center.

Circles: Assorted blue-and-white prints, from scraps to generous ⅛ yard—1 yard total

Background: An assortment of yellows in 4 values, from very light to gold.

2" and 3" blocks: ⅜ yard total of light yellows

4" blocks: ½ yard total yellows

5" blocks: 1¼ yards total deep yellows

6" blocks: ⅝ yard total golds

Note: These are the finished sizes of the blocks.

Batting: 38" x 50"

Backing: 1½ yards

Binding: ½ yard

Additional supplies

Iron-on interfacing: 1 yard

Heat-resistant, clear template plastic: 1 – 12" x 18" sheet

Poster board if template plastic isn't heat-resistant: 1 – 12" x 18" sheet

For the circles, I used lots and lots of blue-and-white prints in many different scales, from tiny, overall designs, to bigger ones that I fussy-cut, to batiks. As I collected prints for this quilt, I took all of them with me to make sure the blues matched. I also looked for fabrics with lots of variety to take advantage of the designs by fussy-cutting them. To give the fabrics a little more body, I added iron-on interfacing to each circle after it was cut. The white interfacing also keeps the backing fabric from shadowing through.

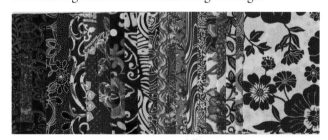

Variety of blue-and-white fabrics.

A border-style print can provide different areas for fussy cutting and appear as more than one fabric.

Note the border-style print on the right.

Cutting and Construction

2" blocks: cut 10 – 2⅞" squares from assorted light yellows. Make 10 half-square triangles to measure 2½" x 2½". (You'll have one extra.)

3" blocks: cut 12 – 3⅞" squares assorted light yellows. Make 12 half-square triangles to measure 3½" x 3½".

4" blocks: cut 16 – 4⅞" squares assorted yellows. Make 16 half-square triangles to measure 4½" x 4½".

5" blocks: cut 20 – 5⅞" squares assorted deep yellows. Make 20 half-square triangles to measure 5½" x 5½".

6" blocks: cut 10 – 6⅞" squares assorted golds. Make 10 half-square triangles to measure 6½" x 6½".

Assemble the entire background to be sure you are happy with the fabric placement. After that, decide on placement of the circles. The whole top is still small enough to manipulate for appliqué, but if you want to do the appliqué in smaller sections simply lay it out, pin the circles in place, do the appliqué on the individual blocks, then assemble. Quilt in an allover circular design.

Cutting the Circles

Use clear template plastic so you can see the image in the fabric that you are framing. If your template material isn't heat-resistant, cut circles from poster board to use when you gather and press your circles to get them ready for stitching. Each of the templates (page 33) is ¾ of the width of its background square. The templates are the finished sizes—leave ⅜" to ½" extra fabric around the edge for gathering the fabric by machine or hand. Once you turn the edge under and press, you can trim the seam allowance if desired.

Circles

2" blocks: cut 9   4" blocks: cut 16

3" blocks: cut 12   5" blocks: cut 20

6" blocks: cut 10

Hand Appliqué

1. Use the templates (page 33) to trace the circles. Cut out adding ⅜" seam allowance.

2. Bond iron-on interfacing to the wrong side of the fabric circle.

3. Run a gathering thread in the seam allowance, by hand or machine, around the edge of circle.

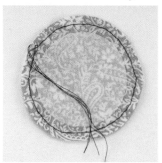

4. Insert a piece of heat-resistant template plastic or poster board in the correct circle size and draw up the gathering stitching.

5. Press the gathered circle smooth and remove the template.

6. Stitch the gathered, pressed circle to the background with small invisible stitches.

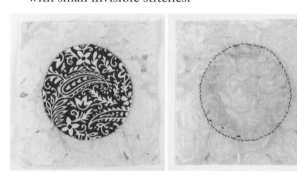

A print not used in the appliqués and cut on the bias would make an interesting binding.

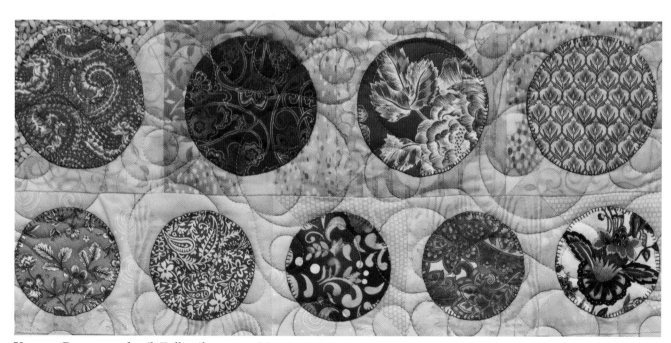

VISIT TO PROVENCE, detail. Full quilt on page 26.

Machine Appliqué

I have to say that I don't like to fuse my fabrics. I love the look of stitching, by hand or machine, plain or decorative. I am also a proponent of traditional methods, and I find it sad that so many quilts are being glued and/or fused together. Fusing as a way to baste before stitching can be all right, but be aware that fusing stiffens your fabric, which will change your options for quilting. Finally, as a desert dweller, I don't trust the glue to last—it dries out, fails, and things fall apart.

But enough about that! Here are some samples of the many options you have for appliqué, and the way I like to do it.

Small zigzag with invisible thread

Small zigzag with blue thread

Running stitch with blue thread

Wide zigzag/satin stitch
with blue thread

Wide zigzag/satin stitch
with yellow thread

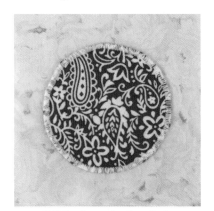

Wide zigzag/satin stitch
with white thread

Blanket stitch with blue thread

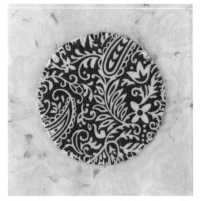

Blanket stitch with white thread

Blanket stitch with yellow thread

THROUGH THE MOONGATE

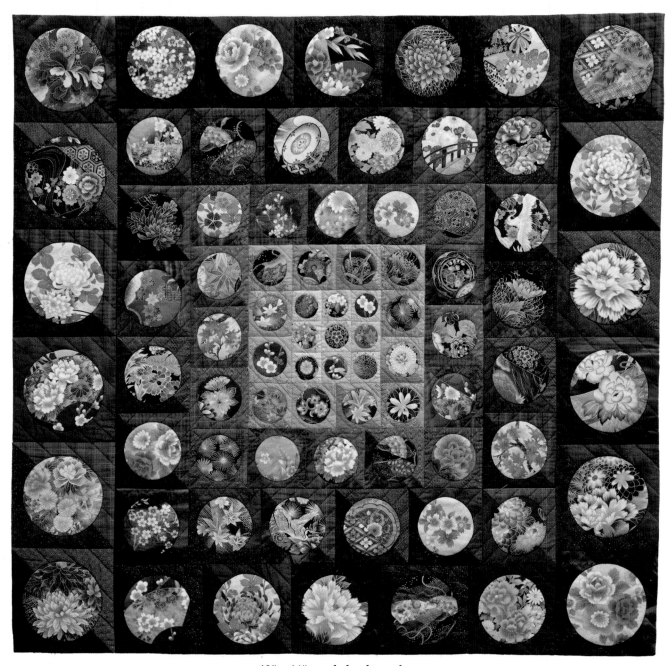

42" x 44", made by the author

This quilt shows another block arrangement for the Graduated grid, as well as another color combination for the circle-in-a-square design. It uses 4 values of taupe, from light to very dark. I used Asian-style prints for the circles. The last "round" consists of 6" squares along the top and bottom and 7" squares along the sides. I added the 7" squares because I wanted some bigger circles.

When you are buying taupe fabrics, you will discover they come with a whole range of undertones from grey to olive to rose. It may take some time to find enough in four values. If you can't find taupes, use a range of browns or grays—either will still look lovely with the Asian prints.

Fabric Requirements

Background: an assortment of taupes in 4 values, from light to very dark:

2" blocks: ⅛ yard total light taupes

3" blocks: ¼ yard total medium-light taupes

4" blocks: ½ yard total medium taupes

5", 6", and 7" blocks: 1¼ yards total EACH medium-dark and dark taupes

These value decisions will be based on the fabrics you find. Rearrange your fabric choices until you are happy with your value progression.

Circles

1½ yards total of a variety of Asian-style prints, some with very large-scale designs

Several fat quarters with big patterns will give you plenty of variety for fussy-cutting your circles.

Iron-on lightweight interfacing

Batting: 50" x 52"

Backing: 3 yards

Facing: ⅜ yard

Cutting and Construction

2" blocks: cut 10 – 2⅞" squares light taupe

3" blocks: cut 12 – 3⅞" squares medium-light taupe

4" blocks: cut 16 – 4⅞" squares medium taupe

5" blocks: cut 20 – 5⅞" squares medium-dark to dark taupe

6" blocks: cut 10 – 6⅞" squares medium-dark to dark taupe

7" blocks: cut 12 – 7⅞" squares medium-dark to dark taupe

Cut the squares in half once on the diagonal and reassemble each group into half-square-triangle blocks. You will have one extra 2" block. Press the blocks and trim the corners.

Circles

2" blocks: cut 9

3" blocks: cut 12

4" blocks: cut 16

5" blocks: cut 20

6" blocks: cut 10

7" blocks: cut 12

Assemble the entire background to be sure you are happy with the fabric placement. After that, decide on the placement of the circles. The whole top is still small enough to manipulate for appliqué, but if you want to do the appliqué in smaller sections, simply lay it out, pin the circles in place, do the appliqué, then assemble.

See Finishing a Quilt with Facing (page 69) for instructions on using a facing instead of binding the quilt.

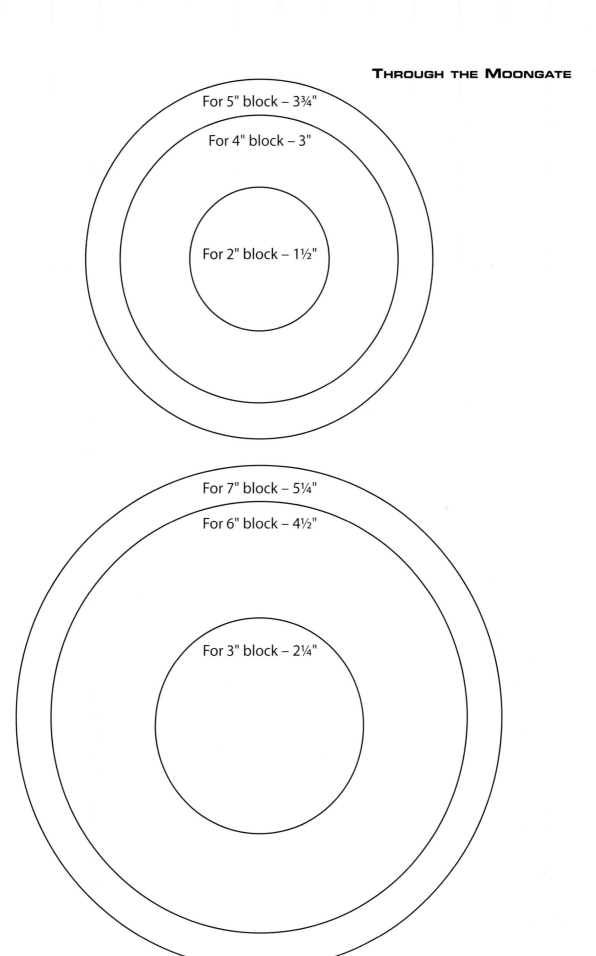

For 5" block – 3¾"

For 4" block – 3"

For 2" block – 1½"

For 7" block – 5¼"

For 6" block – 4½"

For 3" block – 2¼"

Double Sudoku Grid
Sunday Morning Sudoku II

51" x 51", made by the author, quilted by Mary Vaneecke

Working with a Focus Fabric and Eight Colors

I started this Double Sudoku grid quilt with a double puzzle (already solved!), and picked a focus fabric and eight coordinating colors for my nine "numbers." I set off the Nine-Patch blocks with narrow sashing and cornerstones, with black for the sashing (there was black in the focus fabric), some of the eight colors for cornerstones, and the print itself for the large corner areas.

The print in my quilt is contemporary, and any medium- to large-scale pattern with enough color variety can work. To be sure your print has enough colors, see if there's a color key on the selvage. Although those tiny circles are too small for color matching, the number indicates how many different colors were used to print the fabric.

Work with the whole piece of focus fabric and select colors in natural light. One wonderful thing about working this way is working with colors you wouldn't have chosen on your own, but they go together because they are all in the focus fabric.

If the focus fabric includes black and white, choose at least one black-and-white coordinating fabric. Florals can range from traditional to contemporary. Or, pick a theme such as holiday, food, or car fabrics and find an appropriate overall pattern for your sashing and corners.

Sudoku block using food-themed fabrics

Fabric Requirements

1 yard focus fabric

8 coordinating colors

A minimum of 2 – ⅛ yard cuts EACH of 7 different colors (¼ yard TOTAL of each color). More fabrics in each color will provide more visual texture.

2 fat quarters of one color (for the Pinwheel blocks)

¼ yard dark solid for sashing

⅛ yard contrasting color for cornerstones

Batting: 59" x 59"

Backing: 3½ yards

Binding: ½ yard

As you select and assign your colors, remember there will never be two of the same color right beside each other.

Assign block numbers 1–9 to the colors with #1 being the focus fabric. Use at least 2 different fabrics for blocks #2–#9.

Cutting and Block Assembly

Most of the block designs are simple—variations of basic designs, paper-pieced, or simply single squares (Block #1 of the focus fabric). I have included cutting diagrams for the paper-pieced blocks so you can use your fabric more efficiently.

Make 18–19 of each color/block design. The extra blocks will be appliquéd in the large open corners, with some left over. Several blocks are made oversize and trimmed.

The quilt has a total of 153 blocks in the main areas, but it's easy to make them in color groups. The block numbers also indicate the number of pieces in the block (#1 is one square; #9 is a Nine-Patch).

Corner blocks (appliqué background): Cut 2 – 21½" x 21½" squares of focus fabric

Block #1: Cut 17 – 3½" x 3½" squares of focus fabric

Block #2: Cut 18 – 3⅞" squares of at least 2 different fabrics. Cut once on the diagonal and assemble 18 half-square triangles to measure 3½" x 3½".

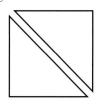

Block #3: Cut 19 – 4½" squares. Follow the cutting and paper-piecing figures.

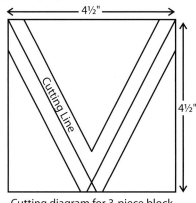

Cutting diagram for 3-piece block
for piecing Block #3

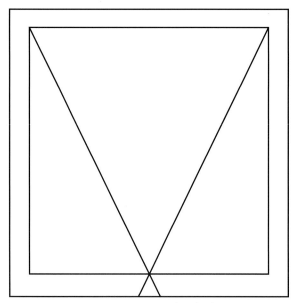

Paper-Piecing Pattern for Block #3
Enlarge 117%

Block #4: Cut 19 – 4½" squares. Follow the diagram for cutting and piecing.

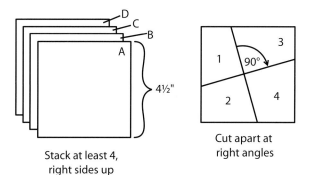

Stack at least 4,
right sides up

Cut apart at
right angles

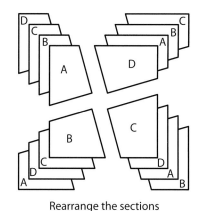

Rearrange the sections

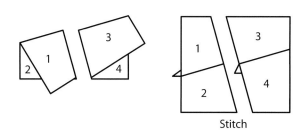

Stitch

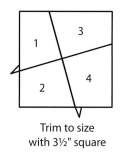

Trim to size
with 3½" square

Block #5: Cut 19 – 4½" squares; use cutting and paper-piecing patterns.

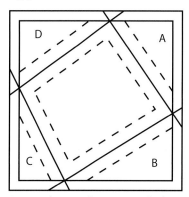

Cutting diagram for piecing Block #5
Enlarge 240%

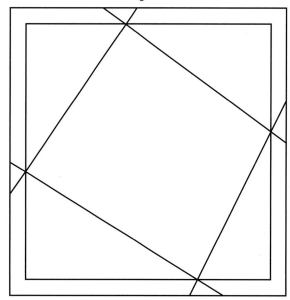

Block #5 Paper-Piecing Pattern
NOTE: Both #5 patterns are reversed   Enlarge 117%

Block #6: Cut 36 – 2" squares and 36 – 2⅜" squares. Cut the 2⅜" squares in half to make 72 half-square triangles.

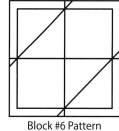

Block #6 Pattern
For each block, join the half-square triangles with the 2" squares.

Block #7: Cut fabrics as shown. Make 19 blocks.

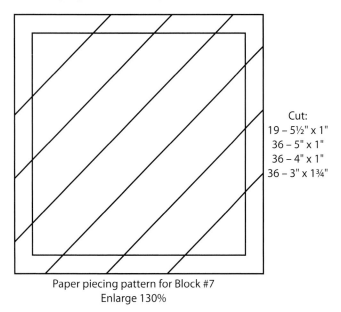

Cut:
19 – 5½" x 1"
36 – 5" x 1"
36 – 4" x 1"
36 – 3" x 1¾"

Paper piecing pattern for Block #7
Enlarge 130%

Block #8: Cut 20 – 5½" squares. Pair two different fabrics, mark, sew, and cut apart as shown. Reassemble into pinwheels. Trim to measure 3½" x 3½".

If you want to cut the pinwheels off-center after assembly, start with 6" x 6" squares.

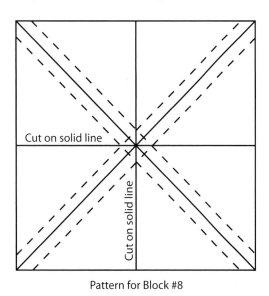

Cut on solid line

Cut on solid line

Pattern for Block #8

Cut 20 – 5½" squares. Draw 2 lines from corner to corner
stitch ¼" each side of drawn lines. Cut apart, and re-piece
into pinwheels, and trim to measure 3½" x 3½".

Block #9: Cut 18 – 4½" squares; piece two blocks at a time, according to the diagram. These blocks are easily made in pairs so cut even numbers of squares.

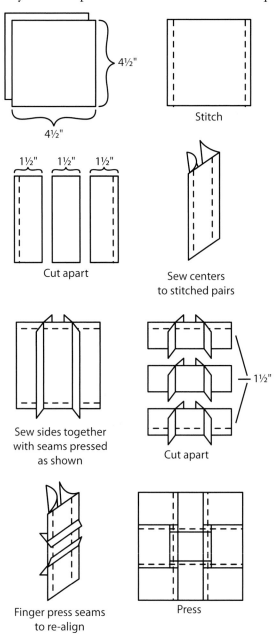

4½"

4½"

Stitch

1½"   1½"   1½"

Cut apart

Sew centers
to stitched pairs

Sew sides together
with seams pressed
as shown

1½"

Cut apart

Finger press seams
to re-align

Press

Assemble the blocks into 17 nine-block sets following the numbers in the block placement and quilt assembly (page 39).

Sashing, Cornerstones, and Quilt Assembly

For the inner sashing, cut:

32 narrow sashing strips, 1" x 9½"

14 – 1" x 1" inner cornerstones

For the wider outer sashing, cut:

12 – 3" x 9½" strips

2 – 3" x 3" cornerstones

12 – 1" x 3" outer cornerstones

Arrange the corner squares, nine-block sets, sashing strips, and cornerstones according to the Color Placement & Assembly Diagram.

Join the units into rows and join the rows in sections, then join the sections to complete the assembly.

Appliqué the extra blocks either before or after the quilting.

Quilt and bind.

Large Double Sudoku: Color Placement & Assembly Diagram

Sudoku Times Three:
Chile con Sudoku

CHILE CON SUDOKU, 26" x 57",
made by the author,
quilted by Mary Vaneecke

This triple arrangement uses plain squares for the blocks and is made on a smaller scale. It would work especially well for starting from a focus fabric, although I must confess I made all the blocks first, then found a fabric to go with them.

Fabric Requirements
⅛ yard total of EACH of 9 colors
Use more than one fabric per color for extra visual interest.
¼ yard Nine-Patch block sashing
⅛ yard cornerstones
½ yard setting triangles (Select one of the colors in the focus fabric.)
¼ yard setting triangle sashing (Select one of the colors in the focus fabric.)
⅝ yard focus fabric (for the border)
34" x 65" batting
2 yards backing
½ yard binding (Select one of the colors in the focus fabric.)

For the Nine-Patch block sashing, I used black, which I made sure to have in the border fabric. The cornerstones are red, my favorite, which is also in the border fabric. If your border doesn't have black, use a dark brown, dark gray, or navy for the sashing. Pick another color from the border for the cornerstones.

Cutting and Assembly
Cut 25 – 2" x 2" squares from each of the 9 colors (225 squares total) for the Sudoku blocks.
Cut 64 – ¾" x 5" strips for the Nine-Patch block sashing.
Cut 40 – ¾" x ¾" squares for the cornerstones.
Cut 2 – 12" x 12" squares twice on the diagonal for the side setting triangles

Cut 2 – 10" x 10" squares once on the diagonal for the corner setting triangles.
Cut 4 – 1¼" x 15" strips for the corner setting triangle sashing.
Cut 8 – 1½" x 10" strips for the side setting triangle sashing.
Cut 3 – 3½" x width-of-fabric strips for the side borders.
Cut 2 – 5½" x width-of-fabric strips for the top and bottom borders.

Assemble the 2" squares into 25 Nine-Patch blocks following the block placement and quilt assembly diagram, labeling each block as you go.

Lay out the cornerstones, ¾" sashing strips, and Nine-Patch blocks into units according to the block placement and assembly diagram (page 42).

Blocks A–F   Blocks G–K
Blocks L–N   Blocks O–S
Blocks T–Y

Add sashing strips to the side and corner setting triangles.

Join the units and setting triangles, using a partial seam as indicated. Trim the sides straight with your longest ruler.

Join the 3 – 3½" border strips. Measure the quilt length; cut 2 strips to that measurement and add to the sides.

Measure the quilt width including the side borders; cut the 5½" strips to that measurement and add to the top and bottom.

Quilt with an allover chile design and bind.

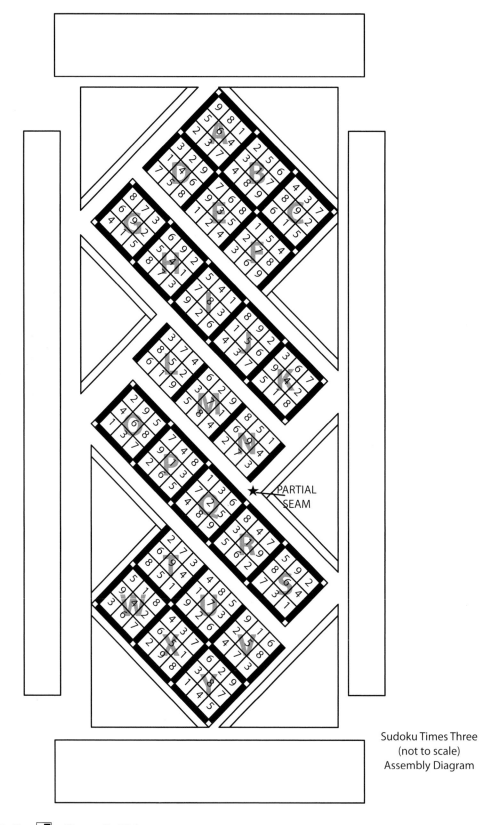

Sudoku Times Three
(not to scale)
Assembly Diagram

PARTIAL
SEAM

SUDOKU IN THE AFTERNOON II

21" x 21", made by the author

This is not a true miniature—the squares are not quite small enough as compared to the original. However, its dimensions do fit within the standard size generally specified for miniatures in quilt shows. The Nine-Patch groups are defined with decorative stitching done as part of the quilting, rather than with sashing.

The buttons add an extra layer of detail and sparkle. They are arranged in groups of four, with some groups straddling the decorative stitching. They are sewn on after the quilting and binding are finished.

Materials

⅜ yard focus fabric
1 fat ⅛ EACH of 9 different colors for the squares
⅛ yard EACH of 2 different fabrics for the narrow
 inner borders
Batting: 25" x 25"
Backing: ¾ yard
Binding: ¼ yard (can be either of the narrow inner
 border fabrics)
17 buttons EACH ½" or smaller to match the 9
 colors of the squares (153 total)

As you are buying buttons in all nine colors, you will discover that some colors are easier to match than others. As the cost of 153 buttons can be a little daunting, I like to wait for button sales at my local fabric store. Many quilt shops are carrying less expensive button assortments of coordinated colors. Also check at local craft stores and "big box" stores—they sometimes carry inexpensive bags of assorted buttons in their craft or scrapbooking departments. (See Resources, page 78.)

Shirting style buttons with holes rather than shanks will lie nice and flat against your quilt. You may also find buttons with small or rounded shanks that work well. It is possible to cut the shank off of a button and drill holes in it with a Dremel® tool and a small craft bit.

Cutting and Construction

Assign numbers to the 9 colors.

From EACH of the 9 color fabrics, cut:
17 – 1½" x 1½" squares (153 total)

From the focus fabric, cut:
2 – 6" x 6" for the corner squares.
4 – 2¾" x 23" strips for the outer border

From EACH of the 2 inner border fabrics, cut:
2 – ¾" x 7" strips (4 total)
2 – ¾" x 6½" strips (4 total)
4 – ¾" x 18" strips (8 total)
These will be trimmed to fit after they are assembled.

Join the 1½" squares into 17 Nine-Patch blocks, matching the numbers assigned to your colors with the numbers in the block placement and quilt assembly diagram.

Add 2 – ¾" x 6½" narrow border strips to 2 adjacent sides of both 6" focus fabric squares. Trim the excess fabric.

Add 2 – ¾" x 7" narrow border strips to 2 adjacent sides of both 6" focus fabric squares. Trim the excess fabric.

Join the bordered squares and Nine-Patch blocks as shown in the assembly diagram.

Add the two narrow borders to the sides and then to the top and bottom of the quilt top.

Add the outer borders, mitering the corners.

Bias binding is the same fabric as in the inner border.

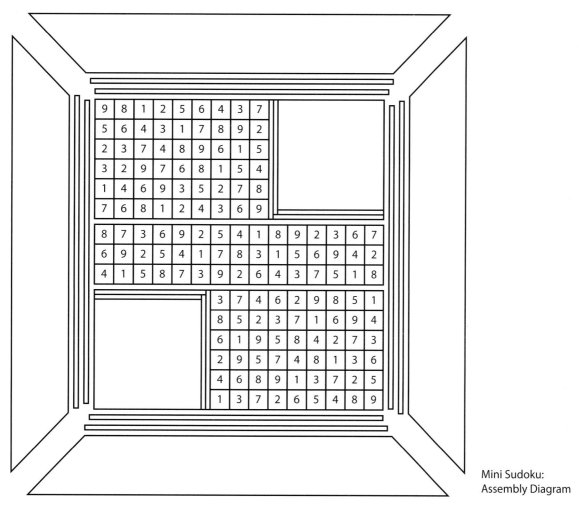

Mini Sudoku:
Assembly Diagram

The quilting is stitched in the ditch for the inner squares and narrow inner borders. The corner squares have a scallop pattern and the quilting in the outer borders follows the design in the focus fabric. Add 2 rows of blanket stitch, back-to-back, to define each Nine-Patch section.

Sew the buttons starting from the front for accurate placement. Stitch through to the back for proper support. After knotting the thread on the back, run it through the batting a short distance to bury the ends of the thread, just as you would in hand quilting.

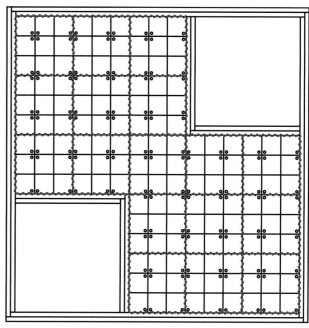

Mini Sudoku: Button & Stitching Placement

Miriam's Grid
Color Progression #1:
INTERFERENCE

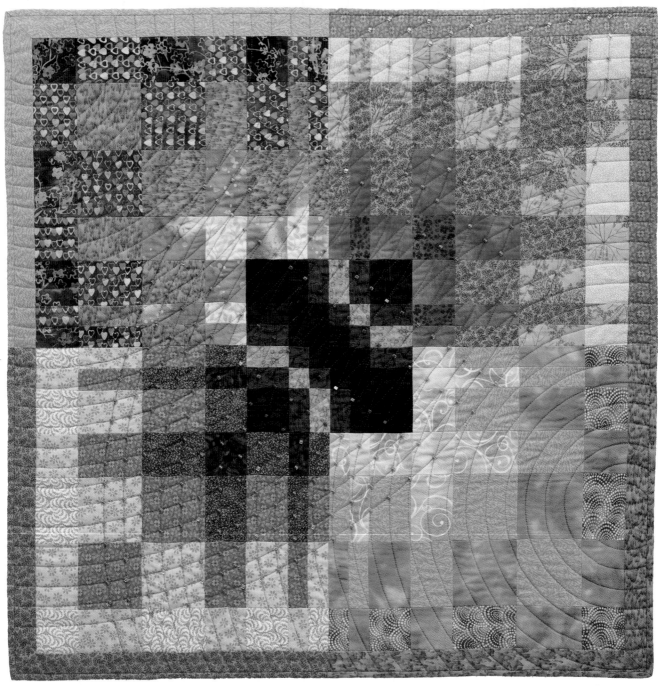

29" x 29", made by the author

Karen G. Fisher

My daughter, Miriam, designed a quilt for herself that she wanted me to make. We shopped together for fabrics, and she chose all solids and marbled fabrics because her design idea was all about color. The blocks were modular and ranged from 3" x 3" to 9" x 9". After I finished her quilt, I tried my own color variations with a smaller version of her grid. I created two more grid variations and started fitting in colors, using the tone-on-tone fabrics I enjoy so much.

At first glance, many people think this is a bargello quilt, but the pieces are changing size in both directions, rather than being made of identical strips that are shifted vertically. When I make it, I find it easiest to cut all the pieces, lay them out, then stitch them together by rows or in small sections.

Most of the versions I have made of this quilt have four to five values (from lightest to darkest) in groups of colors. Variation 3 uses 15 colors that follow the color wheel plus three extra to add variety and value.

This is the basic grid (variation 1). I used five each of four analogous colors on the corners: pink, peach, red-violet, and blue-violet. The center is in four shades of red, the center of this analogous group. The quilting design, which gives the quilt its name, is based on a wave interference pattern.

Materials
⅛ yard EACH of 5 values of pink
⅛ yard EACH of 5 values of peach
⅛ yard EACH of 5 values of red-violet
⅛ yard EACH of 5 values of blue-violet
⅛ yard EACH of 4 values of red
All this adds up to 3 yards of fabric. For a small quilt, I always suggest you start with your stash and build from there.

Batting: 36" x 36" batting
Backing: 1 yard backing
Binding: Match the border as explained below.
5mm cube-shaped beads (amounts are approximate)
2 dozen peach, 3 dozen red, 4 dozen pink, 275 violet

Cutting and Construction
Cut the borders and binding strips first and set them aside. The binding should match the border:
2 strips 1½" x 18" (border) from the middle value of EACH group except red (8 total)
2 strips 1¼" x 18" (binding) from the middle value of EACH group except red (8 total)
Note that the red-violet strips are for the border of the blue-violet section of the quilt and vice versa. In the same way, the pink and peach strips are opposite their sections of the quilt.

Cut the pieces according to the sizes and values shown in the cutting diagram (page 48). Lay out all the pieces. This is a small quilt, but you will need to cut efficiently.

Sew the pieces together row by row, or in the small sections shown in the assembly diagram (page 48), placing the blue-violet opposite the red-violet and the pink opposite the peach. Add the border strips, mitering the corners.

Bind with straight cut binding to match the border fabrics.

Sew a bead by hand at each intersection of the overlapping circles of the quilting design. If the intersections are close enough, run the thread through the batting from one bead to the next.

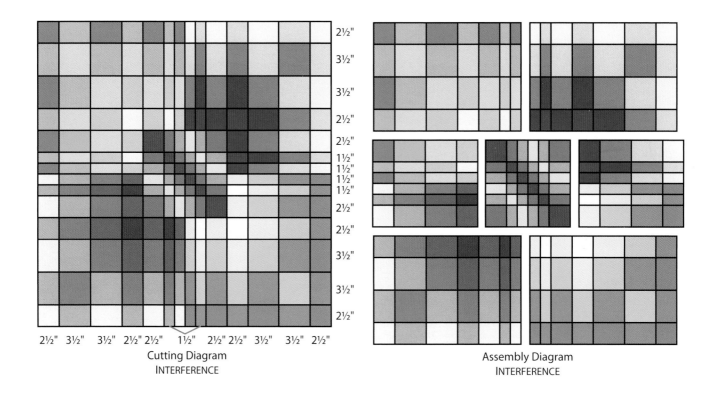

Cutting Diagram
INTERFERENCE

2½" 3½" 3½" 2½" 2½" 1½" 2½" 2½" 3½" 3½" 2½"

2½"
3½"
3½"
2½"
2½"
1½"
1½"
1½"
1½"
2½"
2½"
3½"
3½"
2½"

Assembly Diagram
INTERFERENCE

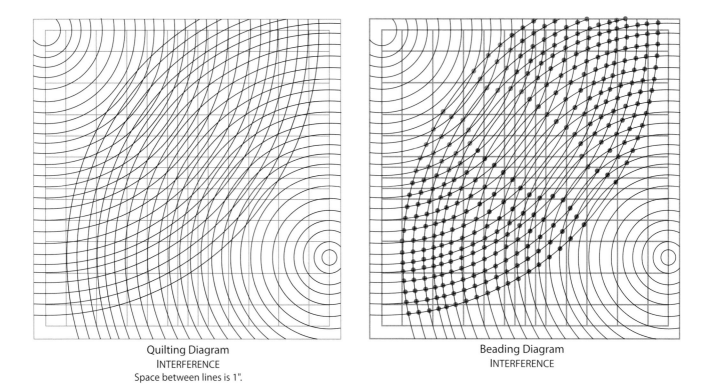

Quilting Diagram
INTERFERENCE
Space between lines is 1".

Beading Diagram
INTERFERENCE

Color Progression #2:
SPARKLING CITRUS SORBET

30" x 30", made by the author

This is the second variation of Miriam's grid and has an extra 1" row of pieces going both directions across the center. I used four values of each color. The borders match the colors as they come to the edge and they are cut from the second lightest value of each color.

Yardage, Cutting, and Assembly
Values of each color are 1-4, from lightest to darkest.

Green: ⅛ yard EACH of four values (½ yard total)
Orange: ⅛ yard EACH of four values (½ yard total)
Yellow: ⅛ yard EACH of the two lightest values and ¼ yard EACH of the two darker values (¾ yard total)
Backing: 1 yard
Batting: 36" x 36"
Binding: ⅜ yard yellow value #3
#10 seed beads

Seed beads are sold in bags or tubes, not by count. Your local bead shop may be able to give you approximate counts on their packages.

Cut a total of 43" of 1½" wide strips of the second lightest value of each color. Set aside for borders.

Use the sizes on the cutting diagram to cut and lay out all the pieces. This is a small quilt, but you will need to cut efficiently.

Sew the pieces together row by row, then assemble the rows.

Add the borders, piecing them along each side to match colors with the center. Miter the corners. Cut 1¼" bias binding strips from the 13" square of yellow value #3 fabric.

The quilting is simply a meandering pattern that moves across the whole surface.

Beads are sewn on after the quilting and binding have been completed. The beads are close enough together to run the thread through the batting between them.

Cut Size	Green Value (Number to Cut)	Yellow Value (Number to Cut)	Orange Value (Number to Cut)
1½" x 1½"	#1(1)	#1 (5), #2 (6), #3 (7), #4 (6)	
1½" x 2½"	#1 (8), #2 (8), #3 (1), #4 (1)	#1 (6), #2 (5), #3 (12), #4 (10)	#1 (2), #2 (2), #3 (3), #4 (2)
1½" x 3½"	#1 (7), #2 (7), #3 (1)	#1 (3), #2 (2), #3 (3), #4 (4)	#1 (6), #2 (6), #3 (1)
2½" x 2½"	#1 (3), #2 (4), #3 (3), #4 (1)	#1 (1), #2 (3), #3 (5), #4 (6)	#1 (2), #2 (3), #3 (3), #4 (2)
2½" x 3½"	#1 (2), #2 (4), #3 (5), #4 (3)	#1 (2), #2 (2), #3 (7), #4 (7)	#1 (5), #2 (6), #3 (3), #4 (2)
3½" x 3½"	#3 (2), #4 (2)	#1 (1), #2 (1), #3 (2), #4 (3)	#1 (1), #2 (1), #3 (2), #4 (1)
Total	63	109	53

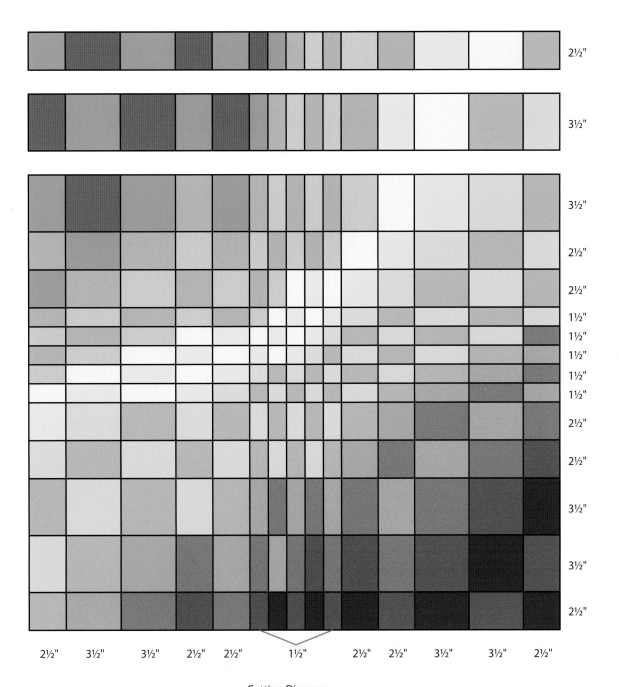

2½"

3½"

3½"

2½"

2½"

1½"

1½"

1½"

1½"

1½"

2½"

2½"

3½"

3½"

2½"

2½" 3½" 3½" 2½" 2½" 1½" 2½" 2½" 3½" 3½" 2½"

Cutting Diagram
SPARKLING CITRUS SORBET
Center is 5 x 5 - 1" squares

Color Progression #3:
Prism II

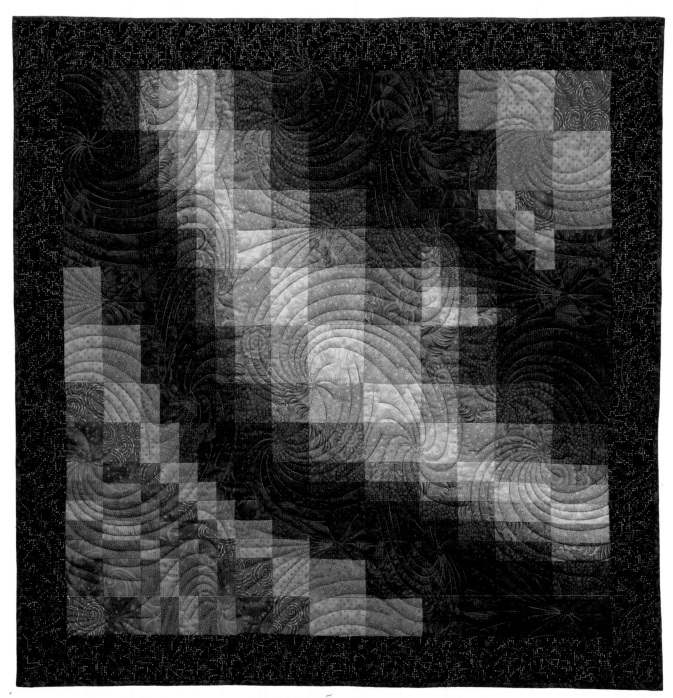

34" x 34", made by the author, quilted by Mary Vaneecke

In variation #3, the smallest part of the grid is moved off-center, and another group of the smallest squares is inserted in another area to balance it. I used 15 colors of fabrics to have smooth color transitions. Many of the "blender" fabrics made by the commercial fabric companies would work wonderfully for this pattern, or find your own selection of tone-on-tone fabrics. The border is a small-scale print that has many of the colors in it, plus black.

I think this quilt would also look wonderful in pastels. For pastels, select a border with a white or light background.

Yardage, Cutting, and Assembly

⅛ yard EACH of 15 colors
½ yard border
Batting: 42" x 42"
Backing: 1¼ yards
Binding: ⅜ yard in one of the 15 colors

Number each of your colors.

Color #1, the bright yellow, is in the center, with the rest following color wheel order as they move out from it. Remember, by putting yellow in the center, it is automatically the visual focus, so the rest of the quilt doesn't have to overcome it.

Use the sizes on the cutting diagram (page 54) to cut and lay out all the pieces. This is a small quilt, but you will need to cut efficiently.

Piece the section of 1" squares in the top right corner. Assemble them with the larger rows they fit into. Piece the rest of the rows and assemble them with the first pieced section.

Cut 4 border strips 2¾" x 34" and add to the quilt top, "spinning" the corners. I find this adds an interesting detail without mitering. (See page 11.)

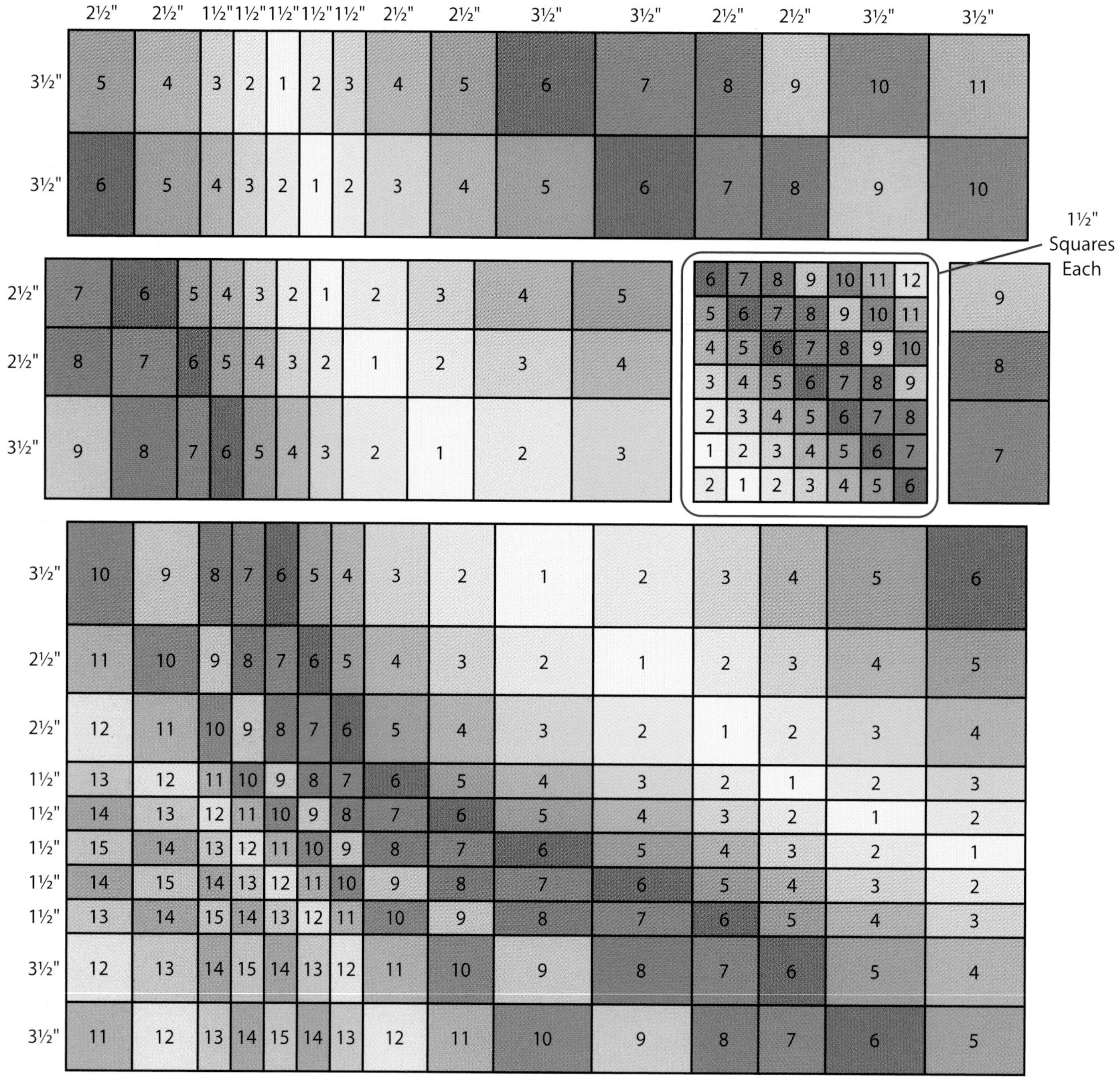

	2½"	2½"	1½"	1½"	1½"	1½"	1½"	2½"	2½"	3½"	3½"	2½"	2½"	3½"	3½"
3½"	5	4	3	2	1	2	3	4	5	6	7	8	9	10	11
3½"	6	5	4	3	2	1	2	3	4	5	6	7	8	9	10

2½"	7	6	5	4	3	2	1	2	3	4	5
2½"	8	7	6	5	4	3	2	1	2	3	4
3½"	9	8	7	6	5	4	3	2	1	2	3

1½" Squares Each

6	7	8	9	10	11	12
5	6	7	8	9	10	11
4	5	6	7	8	9	10
3	4	5	6	7	8	9
2	3	4	5	6	7	8
1	2	3	4	5	6	7
2	1	2	3	4	5	6

9
8
7

	2½"	2½"	1½"	1½"	1½"	1½"	1½"	2½"	2½"	3½"	3½"	2½"	2½"	3½"	3½"
3½"	10	9	8	7	6	5	4	3	2	1	2	3	4	5	6
2½"	11	10	9	8	7	6	5	4	3	2	1	2	3	4	5
2½"	12	11	10	9	8	7	6	5	4	3	2	1	2	3	4
1½"	13	12	11	10	9	8	7	6	5	4	3	2	1	2	3
1½"	14	13	12	11	10	9	8	7	6	5	4	3	2	1	2
1½"	15	14	13	12	11	10	9	8	7	6	5	4	3	2	1
1½"	14	15	14	13	12	11	10	9	8	7	6	5	4	3	2
1½"	13	14	15	14	13	12	11	10	9	8	7	6	5	4	3
3½"	12	13	14	15	14	13	12	11	10	9	8	7	6	5	4
3½"	11	12	13	14	15	14	13	12	11	10	9	8	7	6	5

Cutting Diagram
PRISM II

Triaxial Color Grid
GARLAND

46" x 46", made by the author, quilted by Mary Vaneecke

Before I became interested in quilting, I did ceramics. I took several semesters of classes at the university level, and along the way I learned many glaze-making techniques.

One method used a triaxial blending chart to develop new glazes. The chart outlined how to blend three ingredients in different percentages by weight. After adding water to the dry mix, the glaze was applied to clay and fired. The resulting glazes might or might not be useful.

I wondered if I could use three colors of fabric, mix them in percentages for each block in a grid, and develop a new way to work with color. There were adaptations needed—the basic chart was a triangle, so I made it a right triangle, and mirrored two triangles to make a square. I divided each block into ten equal strips, with each strip representing 10 percent of the whole block. The blocks are 5"square, and each strip of fabric is cut 1" x 5½". I chose three of my favorite colors—red, golden yellow, and turquoise—and went to work.

As that first trial piece came together, I was delighted with how the color moved across the 64-square grid. That first experiment became part of the larger quilt AND THEN THERE'S RED (page 76). I have since made many quilts using this grid. It's especially good as a background for appliqué, yet it is also graphically effective by itself.

Fabric
Choosing Colors
Select 3 colors. Decide which one you want to repeat in opposite corners of the quilt top (Color A). You'll need less of the remaining 2 colors (Colors B & C).

The 3 colors need to have strong contrast for the color patterning to show. I found this out for myself when I made one piece with pink, light yellow, and peach. The colors were very pretty together, but without any value contrast the color patterning simply didn't show.

If you use a color wheel, any triadic color selection will work well. You can also begin with a focus fabric that has good contrast, then choose three colors from it. Again, look for strong value or color change.

Focus fabric with 3 coordinating fabrics

In most cases, I pick three really high contrast colors to work together. However, in all of these samples, you could start by selecting a neutral from the print plus two other colors.

Fabric Requirements

I recommend at least 10 fabrics EACH of the 3 colors—more fabrics will add more visual texture.

Color A:
¼ yard EACH of 4 fabrics
⅛ yard EACH of 6 fabrics
Color B:
¼ yard EACH of 2 fabrics (for both blocks and the outer border)
⅛ yard EACH of 8 different fabrics
Color C:
¼ yard EACH of 2 fabrics (for both blocks and the outer border)
⅛ yard EACH of 8 different fabrics

1¼ yards focus fabric for inner border and motifs for appliqué
1 yard iron-on interfacing
Batting: 54" x 54"
Backing: 3¼ yards
Binding: ½ yard

Cutting and Assembly

The basic quilt has 64 blocks in a Rail Fence layout. Each block is made of 10 rectangular strips.

From EACH of the quarter yard cuts, cut 1 – 3½" x 24" strip for the borders (4 total Color A, 2 each Colors B & C) and set aside.

Color A fabrics:
Cut 34 – 1" x width-of-fabric (WOF) strips into 232 – 1" x 5½" rectangles

Color B fabrics:
Cut 30 – 1" x WOF strips into 204 – 1" x 5½" rectangles
Color C fabrics:
Cut 30 – 1" x WOF strips into 204 – 1" x 5½" rectangles
Focus fabric:
Cut 4 – 1½" x WOF strips for the inner border. The remaining focus fabric will be used for *broderie perse* appliqué.

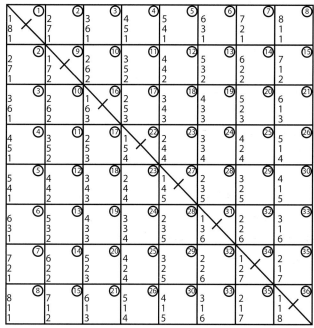

Strip distribution of strips A B C per block

There are 36 different arrangements (indicated by the circled numbers) of the 10 rectangle strips required for each block. The blocks along the marked diagonal are unique. There are 2 blocks for all the other arrangements.

The numbers along the side of each block show how many strips of each color are needed. For example, for arrangement 1 in the upper left corner, you'll need 1 Color A strip, 8 Color B strips, and 1 Color C strip.

The color placement diagram (page 59) shows how the strips are arranged within each block.

The trick to making this quilt come together easily is fabric organization. After cutting the strips, lay out all the stacks of strips in rows, A at the top, B in the center, and C at the bottom.

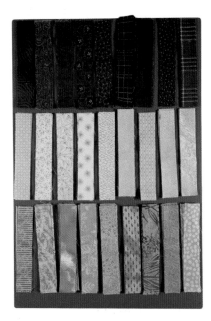

Using the strip distribution diagram that shows the number of strips of each color per block, select the appropriate number and pin them together.

I like to pin the strips for all 64 blocks at once and organize them in zipper bags by rows.

Use the color placement diagram to assemble each of the blocks. Press all the seams in one direction on each block. Join the blocks into rows as each group of eight blocks is completed, which is the easiest way to keep them in order.

After blocks are assembled, add the inner and outer borders, spinning the corners (see page 11).

Broderie Perse

Broderie perse is an appliqué technique in which printed images from one fabric are cut out, rearranged, and stitched to a background fabric. For GARLAND, I selected a fabric that had clearly defined images that would be easy to cut out. Any hand or machine appliqué method will work, but I do not recommend fusing because the texture of all the seams in the background will show through.

I like to give my appliqué pieces some extra body. I rough-cut the shapes I want and back them with fusible interfacing, available at regular fabric stores. After bonding, I outline-cut the images, arrange them as I choose, and pin them in place. For GARLAND, I appliquéd them on with invisible thread and a small zigzag stitch.

Quilt as desired. An allover pattern works well, or you can outline quilt the appliqué, then select a background filler for the rest.

For my bias binding, I used several of the fabrics in Color A, the coral red.

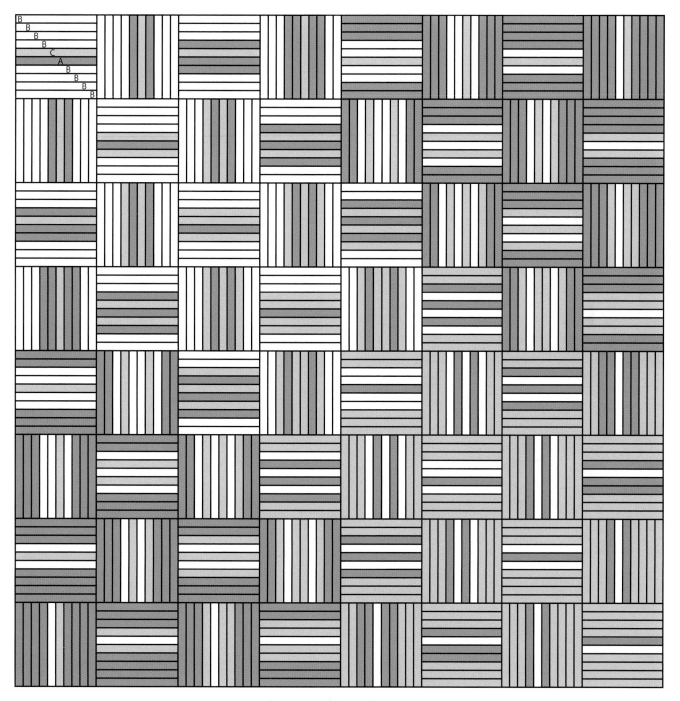

GARLAND and INDIGO ELEGANCE
Color Placement

Color Key: Fabric A (rose or coral red)
              Fabric B (ivory or taupe)
              Fabric C (blue or indigo)

INDIGO ELEGANCE

55" x 55", made by the author, quilted by Mary Vaneecke

At a quilt show a few years ago, I bought a whole selection of traditional indigo fabrics. The vendor had also started carrying a variety of taupe fabrics, and seeing the two together inspired me to combine them in a quilt. I chose a third color, dark red, so I could combine them in my Triaxial grid pattern. I also chose to try a variation of the grid that used graduated sashing between the blocks.

Traditional indigo fabrics have lots of extra dye. Just like new jeans, they will bleed large amounts of blue dye into the water and onto any other fabrics washed with them. They are also loosely woven, so if you buy true indigos, carefully follow the pre-washing instructions that come with the fabric or they will ravel badly. (See Resources, page 78, for indigo dealers.) Note that if you are using traditional indigos, you may need more yardage than called for. They are narrower than standard quilting cottons.

Fabric Requirements

For this quilt, Color A is dark red, Color B is light taupe, and Color C is indigo. Cutting and color placement is the same as with GARLAND (see figure, page 59). The main difference between them is that here the blocks are separated by sashing and cornerstones.

Use as many different fabrics in each color as you can find to give the quilt lots of visual texture and variety.

1¾ yards total of a variety of dark reds (Color A)

1½ yards total of a variety of light taupes (Color B)

1½ yards total of a variety of indigo-colored fabrics (Color C)

The sashing and cornerstones are two darker browns.

½ yard brown (sashing)

1 fat quarter brown print (cornerstones)

1½ yards striped fabric (inner border)

1¾ yards (outer border)

Batting: 63" x 63"

Backing: 3¾ yards

Binding: ½ yard binding

Cutting Instructions

Color A fabrics: Cut 34 – 1" x WOF strips into 232 – 1" x 5½" rectangles

Color B fabrics: Cut 30 – 1" x WOF strips into 204 – 1" x 5½" rectangles

Color C fabrics: Cut 30 – 1" x WOF strips into 204 – 1" x 5½" rectangles

Cut 4 – 1½" x WOF strips for the inner border

Sashing: All pieces are cut 5½" long. Cut 16 in each width (112 total):

1", 1⅛", 1¼", 1⅜", 1½", 1⅝", 1¾"

Cornerstones: Cut 7 cornerstones in each width. Each group can be cut from an 11" strip.

Strip Width	Cut Cornerstone Size
1"	1⅛", 1¼", 1⅜", 1½", 1⅝", 1¾"
1⅛"	1⅛", 1¼", 1⅜", 1½", 1⅝", 1¾"
1¼"	1⅛", 1¼", 1⅜", 1½", 1⅝", 1¾"
1⅜"	1⅛", 1¼", 1⅜", 1½", 1⅝", 1¾"
1½"	1⅛", 1¼", 1⅜", 1½", 1⅝", 1¾"
1⅝"	1⅛", 1¼", 1⅜", 1½", 1⅝", 1¾"
1¾"	1⅛", 1¼", 1⅜", 1½", 1⅝", 1¾"

Cut the sashing strips and cornerstones as you are ready for them, so you don't have lots of tiny pieces to keep track of.

Assemble the blocks in rows with sashing strips. As each row is complete, make a row of sashing strips and cornerstones as indicated in the assembly diagram.

Add the borders. For the inner border, I fussy cut 2" strips from striped fabric. When working with stripes this way, be very careful to allow yourself a full ¼" seam allowance. Cut the fabric in a single layer, and line up your ruler in short stretches rather than assuming the stripe is printed absolutely straight. Pin and stitch your border from the border side, so you can see exactly where the seam needs to line up.

Cut the outer borders 4" wide. Sew from the striped border side again, to be sure it lines up. Spin both borders to add corner detail (see page 11).

INDIGO ELEGANCE
Assembly Diagram

Matrix

MATRIX VI–15²

36" x 36", made by the author

Matrix is the simplest grid of all—a square inside another square. What makes it exciting is the flow of color from low contrast to high contrast areas with contrast both in value and color. My Matrix quilts have won awards all over the United States and I was delighted when my first one, Matrix: Color Synergy, was used as the centerpiece of Contemporary Colorations II: Ride the Rainbow, a special exhibit at the 2009 NQA Show in Columbus, Ohio.

My first Matrix quilt was inspired by my memory of mathematical matrices used for addition and multiplication. Although math was never my strong suit, I remembered my fascination with the patterns of numbers that formed across the matrix as the numbers were combined. I wanted to see what would happen if I used colors instead of numbers. I tried several ideas for combining two-colored squares, but I was also constantly aware that I would need a way to keep 676 little blocks organized. Yes—you read it right—the first matrix quilt used twenty-six colors so it had 676 blocks (26 x 26)!

When I settled on the square-within-a-square idea, I tried both piecing and appliqué construction. I settled on hand appliqué because it gave me the look I wanted, it was the easiest to organize and construct, and the inner squares could have lots of variety in shape and size (see detail—the centers are not all identical, nor are they perfect squares).

Matrix: Color Synergy, detail, full quilt on page 66.

Many people have requested a pattern for this quilt, so here is a simplified version as well as the full color range version. The smaller one uses 15 colors, which is the fewest number of colors I have ever used for this design (only 225 squares!). Use either hand or machine appliqué for the finished look you prefer.

Fabrics

⅛ yard, fat eighths, or scraps from your stash of at least 4 fabrics in EACH of 15 colors
¼ yard medium gold & brown print (inner border)
½ yard second medium gold & brown print (outer border)
Batting: 40" x 40"
Backing 1¼ yards
Binding: ¼ yard
1 yard fusible interfacing (if you choose to machine appliqué the squares)

The background colors are listed across the bottom of the color layout diagram and the appliquéd square colors are listed along the right edge.

The color sequence is just like a color wheel, except I have added more values with the yellow and gold, and the two values of red, turquoise, and yellow-green. It seems to me that after making several of these quilts, the more variety I add in value, the better the quilt looks.

Cutting and Construction

For the background columns, cut 15 – 2½" squares of each color. Arrange the fabrics randomly, and sew each column of 15 squares together.

NOTE: Instead of cutting individual squares, you can strip-piece 2½" strips of fabric, then cut and assemble them into full columns of 15 squares, but I like the visual variety of arranging the squares randomly.

For hand appliqué

Assemble the columns in groups of three or four columns, keeping the proper color order.

Cut 15 squares of each color, 1⅜" – 1½" so you can turn the edges under for a finished size of 1" x 1".

Put a square of white fabric behind the light-colored squares going on a dark background before appliquéing so the background won't shadow through.

Appliqué the centers onto each group of columns, being careful to keep the colors in the proper order. After completing the appliqué, sew the columns together.

For machine appliqué

Assemble all the background columns.

Fuse interfacing to enough of the color fabrics to cut 15 – 1" x 1" squares of each color.

Fuse the squares to the background one color at a time and appliqué with either a blanket or satin stitch.

Borders

Cut 4 – 1" x 31" strips from the inner border fabric and add to the center, spinning them in one direction around the quilt (see page 11).

Cut 4 – 2¾" x 33½" strips from the outer border fabric and add to the center, spinning them in the same direction as the inner border.

Note: Make sure your border pieces are the correct length for your quilt. Seam allowances will vary from person to person, so your border may need to be slightly longer or shorter.

Quilting

For the center area, stitch in the ditch to set off the individual squares. Stitch around the inner squares for more detail. Do something a bit fancier in the border, or simply let your quilting follow the pattern of your fabric.

Binding

Any of the colors from the center will work to set off the edge of the quilt. I especially like turquoise binding against the brown border.

Color layout for Matrix VI 15²

MATRIX: COLOR SYNERGY

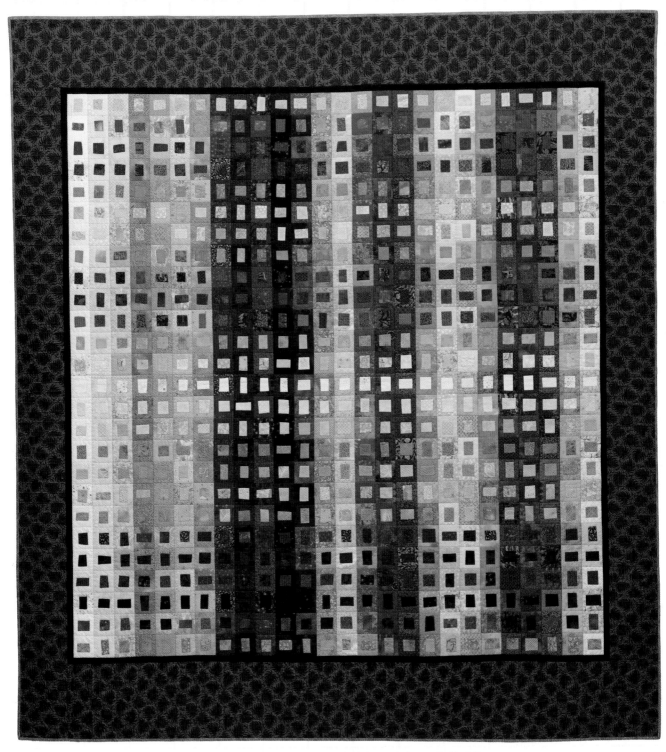

74" x 84", made by the author, quilted by Karolyn "Nubin" Jensen

Karen G. Fisher

For the large version of this design I used 26 different colors. It can be hard to find the colors I had chosen in simple tone-on-tones, so I also looked at multicolored prints. Sometimes, with fussy cutting, I could use areas of color within the overall pattern to provide the colors or values I needed. I also used many fabrics that were basically monochromatic with imagery in them. For example, there are wonderful allover food prints of things like berries and peas, and winter scenes with lots of blues. Many fabrics that have been designed with landscape quilts in mind may also have areas of browns and greens that blend beautifully in small pieces. Larger-scale floral prints will have areas of green and areas of color that can be fussy-cut.

Use the diagram color list to select your 26 colors. Not only are there multiple values of several colors, this bigger matrix also includes neutrals: off-white, beige, black, brown, and dark gray. The neutrals are fit into the color run by value—lights next to lights and darks next to darks. I also really like fabrics with gold in them, so they are scattered throughout.

Fabric Requirements

¼ yard TOTAL of a variety of EACH of 26 different colors
⅜ yard black (inner border)
2 yards brown print (outer border)
Batting: 82" x 92"
Backing: 5⅜ yards
Binding: ⅝ yard

Cutting and assembly

Making this quilt is all about organization. I never drew it out in color—I drew the 26 x 26 square grid, labeled the columns and rows of color, and kept that labeled grid with me as I worked. By assembling three to four columns (vertical strips) of color at a time,

and doing the appliqué for those rows before sewing the next set of columns, I was able to keep track of where I was on the quilt without being overwhelmed by the prospect of having to make 676 –2½" blocks!

For each color, collect all the fabrics you are going to use. The number of fabrics you find per color will determine how many you cut of each one.

Cut 26 – 3" x 3" squares per color. If you choose to do all your cutting at once, simply place the fabrics in zipper bags until you are ready to assemble them.

Stitch together the squares for the first three columns, following the color layout diagram (page 68). Refer to the color layout, and appliqué all the centers. I rough-cut the centers about 1¾" square. When I turned the edges under for appliqué, I allowed the "squares" to vary in size.

Use this same process to join the appliquéd columns in groups of 3–4 columns, adding each multi-column section to the previous section. One of the best parts of making this quilt is seeing the color interactions as they start to happen.

Borders and Binding

Cut inner border strips 1¼" wide; piece as necessary. Add to the center, spinning the corners (page 11).

Cut the top outer border strips 8½" wide and the bottom 9½" wide; piece as necessary. Add to the center.

Cut outer border side strips 6½" wide. Trim as needed.

Quilt as desired and bind with strips 2¼" wide joined with 45-degree seams.

	light blue
	medium blue
	dark blue
	brown
	turquoise
	aqua
	light green
	kelly green
	dark gray
	forest green
	olive green
	dk. yellow-green
	lt. yellow-green
	off-white
	light yellow
	yellow-gold
	orange
	peach
	beige
	pink
	medium red
	dark red
	magenta
	black
	purple
	lavender

Columns (background colors across the bottom): off-white, light yellow, yellow-gold, orange, peach, beige, pink, medium red, dark red, magenta, black, purple, lavender, light blue, medium blue, dark blue, brown, turquoise, aqua, light green, kelly green, dark gray, forest green, olive green, dk. yellow-green, lt. yellow-green

Color Layout: Background colors are listed across the bottom and the appliquéd square colors are listed along the right edge.

Finishing Your Quilt

Finding a Longarm Quilter

If you have not worked with a longarm quilter before, ask at your local quilt shops for names and phone numbers of people in your area. When you go to see the quilters, ask to see some of their previous work. If that is not possible, you might choose to have them quilt a small, simple quilt for you so you can see the quality of their work. Remember, this is your work you're asking them to add to—make sure you are comfortable handing over your quilt top for them to complete.

I have worked with Mary Vaneecke in Tucson on many projects. For some quilts, I have had a clear idea of what I wanted, and on others I let Mary make the choices—a true collaboration. She does her own award-winning quilts, and has worked with clients on a full range of allover patterns as well as custom heirloom quilting to fulfill any client's tastes and needs.

Look at Mary's website at http://maryvaneecke.com to learn a little about her and view her work. She does work long-distance with clients, as well as with a huge number of quilters in Tucson, Arizona.

Bias Binding—a Low-Tech Approach

Finally, the binding! When I began quilting, I immediately began using bias binding because I thought that was the standard. I was also comfortable working with bias from my dressmaking days, and I knew bias could give me a smoother edge on my quilts, as well as go around any shaped edge.

Most new quilters are now encouraged to use straight-cut binding, perhaps because it is easier to cut. However, it can be difficult to make straight-cut binding lie as smoothly as you would like. Bias binding is just as easy to cut with a few simple steps. It lies beautifully along the edge of your quilt and can add that last, perfect accent. If you use a cutting mat, a ruler, and a rotary cutter, you already have all the tools you need to make bias binding.

For all the quilts in this book (except MATRIX: COLOR SYNERGY), ½ yard of fabric will be plenty. On some quilts the binding changes color or fabric as it goes around the edge. If you choose a variegated binding, you will still follow the same directions.

To cut bias binding, line up a corner of your fabric with the horizontal and vertical grid lines on your cutting mat. Line up your ruler with one of the 45-degree lines on the mat and make your first cut. Once the first cut is made, you can fold the cut edge to a manageable size to cut strips: 1¼" for single-fold binding or 2¼" strips for double-fold binding. To make enough binding, I simply lay the strips around my quilt until I have enough. Stitch the ends together, using a short stitch length. On double-fold binding, press the whole strip in half, lengthwise, wrong sides together.

Because bias binding is stretchy, I always pin my bindings in place, stretching them slightly as I go so they will lie smoothly after stitching. Sew one side of the binding in place at a time, stopping and starting at the corners so they turn smoothly. Stitch or overlap the ends and stitch down. Turn the binding to the back and stitch down by hand.

Finishing a Quilt with Facing

As soon as I began making THROUGH THE MOONGATE, I knew I wanted it to have a completely plain edge. The easiest way to achieve this is to use a facing rather than binding. Facing is a method used mostly in clothing. It is invisible from the front and gives a clean, elegant finish to a quilt edge.

For the illustrated steps, I have used a pre-quilted commercial fabric, plus a matching fabric to show how the technique works. Select a fabric that matches the fabric(s) at the edge of your quilt.

Cut enough facing fabric 2" x the length needed to go around your quilt. Piece if necessary to have long enough strips for each side. Cut each side slightly longer than the length of the quilt.

Pin facing strips to opposite sides of the quilt, right sides together. Stitch with ¼" seam allowance (1). Press the strips away from the quilt top (2). Turn the strips to the back and trim the corners at a 45-degree angle (3). Fold under the long edge and pin in place (4). Repeat on the opposite facing.

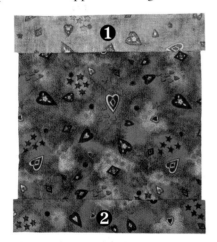

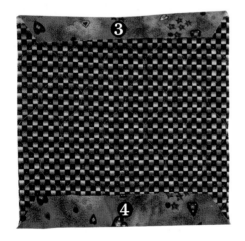

Sew facing strips to the remaining two sides (5). Press (6) and trim the corners (7) as before. Fold under the diagonal and long edges and pin in place (8), covering the raw diagonal edges of the first two facing strips. Hand stitch the facings in place (9).

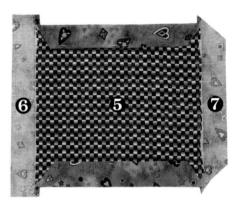

To add an extra detail to the back, give your facing a pretty shaped edge, as I did on THROUGH THE MOONGATE.

THROUGH THE MOONGATE, back detail

Gallery

DREAMING OF AFRICA

42" x 44", made by the author, quilted by Mary Vaneecke

This was the first quilt I made with the basic Graduated grid pattern. I had great fun using African-style fabrics left over from a series of giraffe quilts I had made in the past. The heads were taken from another fabric and are machine appliquéd.

THE COLLECTION

56½" x 56½", made and quilted by Kathryn E. Wald, Tucson, Arizona

I asked my friend Kathryn to make a quilt using the Graduated grid and a "house" theme. She designed many of her own blocks to piece and appliqué, as well as fussy-cutting lots of house fabrics. She surrounded her houses with a 7" Log Cabin border to continue the size progression of the blocks.

KALEIDOSCOPE GARDEN

50" x 50", made by Carol W. Carpenter, Tucson, Arizona, quilted by Mary Vaneecke

KALEIDOSCOPE GARDEN was created using appliquéd flowers, butterflies, and leaves on solid background blocks, and Four-Patch blocks in four colors that coordinate with the appliquéd motifs. The appliquéd blocks are defined by lead line tape to give a stained glass effect. "Karen asked me to create a wall quilt utilizing both her background grid and the stained glass effect." This quilt has already won awards in two shows.

MATRIX II: THERE'S ALWAYS ROOM FOR MORE RED

21" x 21½", made and quilted by the author

My second Matrix was a miniature. The column squares are ½", and the interior squares are handmade paper beads. Seed beads add lots of sparkle.

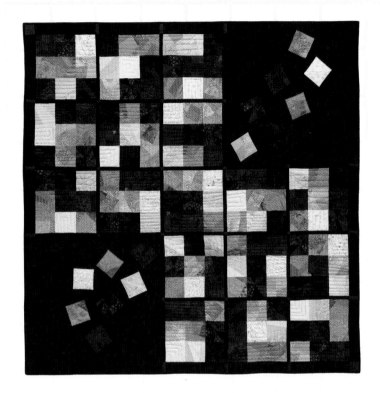

SUNDAY MORNING SUDOKU

51" x 51", made and quilted by the author

This was my very first Sudoku quilt. The black corner areas and the sashing are tucked silk. The colors, from purple through orange, are my all-time favorite group of analogous colors. There are also silks in several of the colors. Notice that there are three values of red, two of purple, and red-orange is represented by peach, a lighter value than the basic hue. The white-and-gold prints work as the lightest value and a neutral.

FLOWERS FROM DRESDEN: LATE BLOOMERS

52" x 52", made and quilted by the author

This quilt was inspired by a Dresden Plate challenge, but I didn't finish it in time—therefore the "late bloomers." The three colors for the Triaxial grid are bright pink, gold, and dark red, with ivory-and-gold prints for the three sizes of Dresden plates. Tucked borders finish the right and bottom edges, with the binding in the same fabric as the flower centers. Beads and metallic thread add sparkle.

ALL BUTTONED UP

30" x 30", made and quilted by the author

This is yet another variation of the Graduated grid. Each block is "spun," with a button to finish off each center. Note the placement of the yellow. Its symmetrical arrangement lets it be the center of attention.

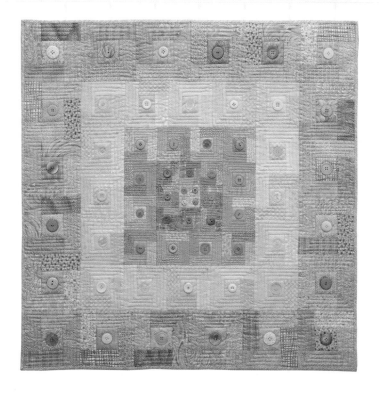

ORNAMENTS

28" x 28", made and quilted by the author

Circles were cut from a large selection of metallic print fabrics. The whole range of colors, including black, was inspired by my mother's favorite black and gold Christmas ornaments. The border, beginning with the narrow red strip, is all cut in one piece from a large Christmas striped pattern. The corners are "spun" to add detail.

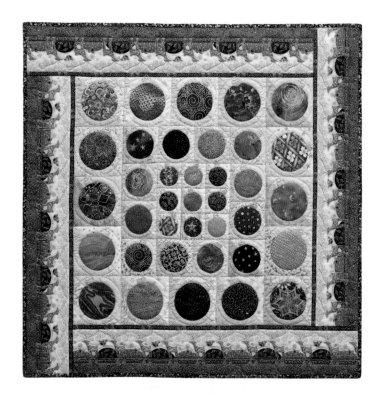

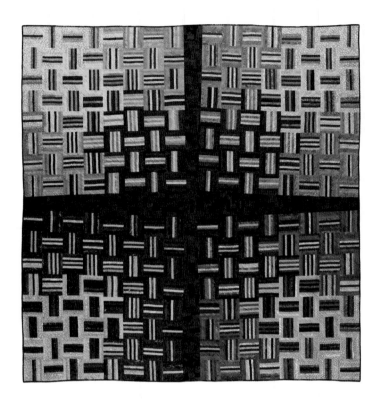

AND THEN THERE'S RED

82" x 82", made and quilted by the author

This quilt combines four separate Triaxial grid combinations. When I tried to put together four different color combinations, I realized that red worked well with all of them. It became the unifying element in the quilt. The randomly pieced section through the middle made the red even more important. It was quilted in four sections, then assembled.

SPIRAL IN, SPIRAL OUT

42" x 42", made and quilted by the author

Black, white, and red are always a dynamic combination. This is the Pieced Blocks variation of the Graduated grid. The red ribbon that follows the block sizes was appliquéd after all the quilting was finished.

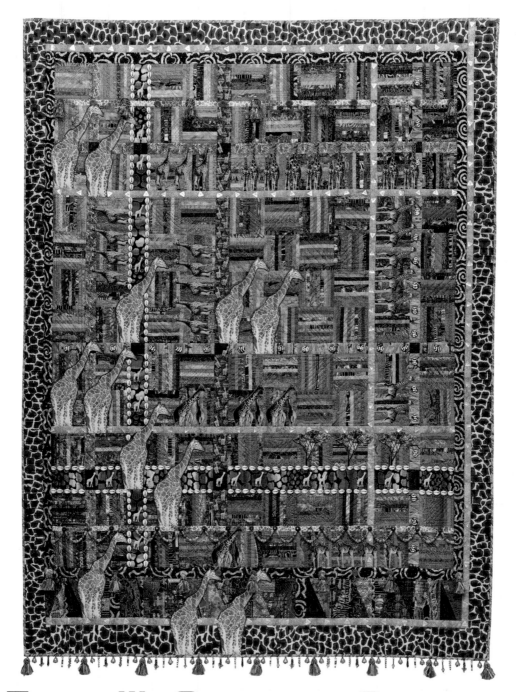

TWIGA III: SAVANNAH SUNLIGHT

67" x 87", pieced and embellished by the author, quilted by Mary Vaneecke

"Twiga" means "giraffe" in Swahili, and this is one of an ongoing series that highlights giraffe imagery. The background Triaxial grid uses gold, green, and a wide assortment of prints, with sashing dividing it into large sections. It is heavily embellished with beads, buttons, and tassels, and both outer borders and some of the sashing strips are tucked.

Resources

I always begin my quilts with fabrics from local quilt and fabric shops. I also enjoy buying unusual fabrics and products from the wonderful vendors who come to my local quilt guild show. Because I live in a large city, I also have easy access to most of the beads, buttons, tassels, and other things I use to embellish most of my quilts. Most of my embellishments are attached after the quilting, and even the binding, are complete.

If you don't have local access to some of these things, here are a few online resources that can help you find all the wonderful things you need to create your quilts.

Indigo Fabrics

Most quilt shops do not carry true indigo fabric. It is more expensive than their regular lines of fabric, and is narrower than the bolt fabric we are all used to, so fabric quantities need to be adjusted for patterns. It also has an odd smell, which you may or may not like. Most of the smell washes out and eventually wears out.

Cotton in the Cabin at www.cottoninthecabin.com carries a large line of indigo fabrics. When you purchase fabric from them, they will send you very good washing instructions, which need to be followed carefully for the best use of the fabric. For INDIGO ELEGANCE (page 60) I purchased two different rolls of fat eighths, and selected the ones I liked best. (There were soccer ball designs, for example, which I chose not to use.)

Buttons

Jill Gorski owns Jillions of Buttons at www. jillionsofbuttons.com. I first met her as a vendor at the Tucson Quilt Fiesta, and she helped supply many of the buttons I used on SUDOKU IN THE AFTERNOON II (page 43). She has wonderful buttons in a wide range of colors and prices.

Many quilt shops will carry some selection of buttons, as embellished wall quilts have become more and more popular. Also try fabric shops, yarn shops, and even the chain super stores.

Assorted Embellishments

In Tucson, a store called Picánte Designs has an amazing assortment of accessories and high-end handmade items, primarily from Mexico, including the painted tin hearts on DREAMING OF NEW MEXICO (page 19). They do not have an online shop because their merchandise changes often, but you can look at the kinds of things they carry on their website at www.picantetucson.com. If you are interested in purchasing items from them, they are happy to help you over the phone at (520) 320-5699.

Beads are available from many craft and fabric stores. Explore your local resources, including "big box" stores that have craft departments. I also buy inexpensive jewelry and take it apart for the beads.

Tassels can be purchased most inexpensively in an upholstery shop or department. Buy tasseled fringe by the yard, and cut it apart. Just make sure the tassels are attached in such a way that they can be cut off cleanly, leaving a loop at the top for sewing them onto your quilt.

Meet Karen G. Fisher

Photo by Howard W. Fisher

I came to quilting as an art form just a few years ago, but I had a lifetime of art-making and sewing as a background to build on. Like many women, I made a quilt for my granddaughter, fell in love with the medium, and let it grow from there. Before quilting my main medium was ceramics, and I feel some of my quiltmaking style has grown out of my ceramics work in terms of building a surface with color, pattern, and texture. I also love to use commercial tone-on-tone fabrics for the visual sparkle they give a piece, and I always enjoy the hunt to find the groups of colors I want for a new quilt.

Besides my ceramics background, one of my favorite sources of inspiration is astronomy—one quilt that toured for a year with an International Quilting Association special exhibit was based on a star classification chart. In both cases I enjoy taking something very structured and giving it a bit of a twist; however, a viewer doesn't need to know either ceramics or astronomy to enjoy the visual impact of my quilts.

I've been really delighted with the awards my quilts have won in Tucson, Phoenix, Salt Lake City, Chicago, Columbus, Ohio, Denver, Houston, and Knoxville. My quilts have been shown in Paducah, Cincinnati, California, and exhibited at both the Rocky Mountain Quilt Museum and The National Quilt Museum. My work has also been shown in *American Quilter*, the *2007 Quilt Art Engagement Calendar*, *Quilting Arts*, and *The Quilting Quarterly*. *Rose of Sharon: New Quilts from an Old Favorite* includes my quilt MY FATHER'S ROSE GARDEN. As an active quilter I am always adding to my skills—I've taken workshops with Carol Taylor, Katie Pasquini-Masopust, Paula Nadelstern, and others.

My formal art training includes a BFA in sculpture from the University of Arizona, plus a BFA in art education, and an earth science teaching endorsement. I have taught both art and science at the high school and middle school levels, and have included quilting in the art curriculum. I've been active with the Tucson Quilters Guild for the last six years, where I was program co-chair and had the opportunity to work with the amazing group of nationally recognized speakers the guild brings to Tucson each year.

More AQS Books

This is only a small selection of the books available from the American Quilter's Society. AQS books are known worldwide for timely topics, clear writing, beautiful color photos, and accurate illustrations and patterns. The following books are available from your local bookseller, quilt shop, or public library.

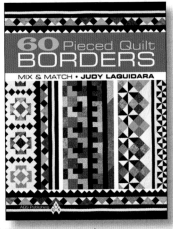
#8662 $26.95

#8242 $22.95

#8665 $19.95

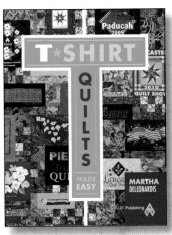
#8664 $19.95

#8523 $26.95

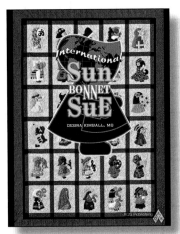
#8347 $24.95

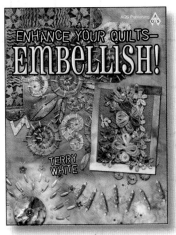
#8532 $26.95

#8529 $26.95

#8349 $24.95

LOOK for these books nationally.
CALL or **VISIT** our website at

1-800-626-5420
www.AmericanQuilter.com